FAMILY
ITALIAN

FAMILY ITALIAN

Simple, Delicious Favorites Made to Share

STERLING EPICURE
New York

To my lovely family

STERLING EPICURE
New York

An Imprint of Sterling Publishing
387 Park Avenue South
New York, NY 10016

First Sterling edition 2013

First published in 2012 by Pavilion Books, an imprint of
Anova Books Company Ltd
10 Southcombe Street
London W14 0RA

ISBN 978-1-4549-1021-3

Distributed in Canada by Sterling Publishing
c/o Canadian Manda Group, 165 Dufferin Street
Toronto, Ontario, Canada M6K 3H6

For information about custom editions, special sales,
and premium and corporate purchases, please
contact Sterling Special Sales at 800-805-5489 or
specialsales@sterlingpublishing.com.

Manufactured in China

2 4 6 8 10 9 7 5 3 1

www.sterlingpublishing.com

Cook's note: all eggs and vegetables are medium
unless otherwise stated

CONTENTS

THE FAMILY THAT COOKS TOGETHER STAYS TOGETHER

Food brings people together. When I was growing up it was the favorite topic of conversation at the dinner table. This was the same table on which my mother would roll out fresh pasta, knead bread dough or bottle preserves. This table was our altar, a place where all members of our family sat to eat, discuss, argue, laugh, sometimes cry — we had the best of times around it. All my family cooked, including my father, who still liked to make his own meals when he was well into his 90s. My aunts, cousins, neighbors, friends, in fact everyone I knew, cooked — the meals weren't elaborate affairs, but this was good, honest family cooking.

When I first came to England in 1969 I found it odd that food was not a priority in people's lives — they mostly liked to grab a quick bite on the go or eat from a plate balanced on their laps. And, horror of horrors, pasta was out of a can! Of course, things have changed dramatically since then — the immigrants to this country have brought their national dishes and foods and we have been exposed to numerous cooking programs on television, cookery books and magazines, enticing us to cook and experiment. More recently, with fears of GM foods and intensive farming, we have turned to organic, natural and seasonal produce. When I was young, we ate mainly locally grown food. Nowadays we can find all sorts of exotic things to eat, flown in from around the globe, but I still prefer to eat seasonally. I look forward to the first broad beans and peaches in summer, and some of my favorite produce in autumn — pears, walnuts and chestnuts.

As a parent, I strongly believe in implementing good eating habits from an early age, and showing my kids where our food comes from and how to cook it. I was taught to respect food; the chickens and rabbits we kept were treated humanely. We never wasted food and leftovers were always used. Now my girls really enjoy making bread, pizza, pasta or gnocchi with me, and baking cakes with their mom. They are fascinated to see what I bring home when I've been out hunting; they are not afraid to touch the game birds and aren't squeamish about watching me clean them. When I was old enough, my father would take me hunting – we only killed for food, never for fun – and he taught me a lot. My mother introduced me to wild herbs and mushrooms; I would go with her to the hills above our village of Minori and she would teach me to identify the different species. Food was all around us and dominated our lives. 'Cosa mangiamo per pranzo?' ('What shall we eat for lunch?') was a constant refrain.

Family life in Italy is changing. More women work outside the home, so they no longer have time to prepare fresh pasta and the other traditional dishes their mothers and grandmothers used to make. However, Italians still want to eat well, and even if their fresh pasta is shop-bought they will still try to ensure it's of good quality. Italians still talk about food a lot and, although their meals might be a little more rushed these days, the family still gets together for the evening meal around a table – and certainly always on Sundays.

It is so easy to buy everything ready-made these days that I think we forget we can actually make it ourselves. Take something as basic as bread; not only do my children and I have fun making the dough, watching it rise and enjoying that magical moment when it is baked, but I also know they are eating something good. For me, this is spending quality time with my family – and I am passing on some of my family traditions, which I hope will stay with them forever.

SOUP

We loved soup as children, especially during the colder months. My older sisters were the experts. They made soup with beans, pulses, vegetables and all sorts of leftovers — even stale bread. It was perfect comfort food, warming and gentle yet satisfying and full of goodness. We always kept different types of legumi (pulses) in small sacks — borlotti, cannellini, black-eyed, kidney and broad beans, peas and lentils. My sisters would patiently sift through them to discard any impurities and then soak them in cold water overnight before cooking them the next day with vegetables and herbs to make the most delicious, hearty soup. I dedicate this chapter to my elder sisters, Filomena, Genoveffa and Carmelina, for being the best soup-makers ever.

In rural Italy it was common for soup to be made early in the morning and left gently bubbling on the stove until everyone came home in the evening. This ensured an instant warm, home-cooked meal.

Soup is sometimes served instead of pasta or risotto as a primo (starter). For the evening meal, a light soup in the form of a vegetable or meat broth (usually chicken or beef) with small pastina shapes, and a good sprinkling of grated Parmesan is quite common. For a more substantial soup, small ravioli or bread dumplings are added. Pastina in brodo (small pasta shapes in broth) is an Italian favorite, and reminds me of home-cooking in my childhood.

Soups are easy to make, nutritious and economical, and they can be made in large quantities to be frozen and then enjoyed when you have little time to cook, making them nutritious 'fast food'. This is a perfect way to use up seasonal vegetables when you get a glut of, say, zucchinis (zucchini), spinach or pumpkin.

I still enjoy soup at home today, and my wife Liz loves to make it — from light pastina broths for the girls and delicate vegetable puréed soups to substantial bean and pasta soups that are a meal in themselves.

Minestra di verdure

Vegetable soup

- - - - - - - - - - - - - - - - - - -

SERVES 4–6

5 tbsp extra-virgin olive oil

1 onion, finely chopped

1 garlic clove, finely chopped

1½ oz/40g pancetta or bacon, finely
chopped (optional)

2 potatoes, peeled and cubed

2 carrots, thickly sliced

1 celery stalk, thickly sliced

1 zucchini, cubed

1 leek, finely chopped

4 cherry tomatoes

3½ oz/100g podded fresh or frozen peas

3½ oz/100g podded fresh or frozen
broad (fava) beans

1½ quarts/1.5 liters vegetable stock

9oz/250g ditalini or other small pasta shape

salt and freshly ground black pepper

a few fresh basil leaves, finely chopped

Parmesan, grated, to serve (optional)

- - - - - - - - - - - - - - - - - - -

There is nothing nicer at the end of a long day than a bowl of homemade vegetable soup. I usually throw in whatever fresh vegetables I have, plus frozen peas and broad (fava) beans, which I always keep (of course, in season, it is better to use these fresh, but if you do, add them with the rest of the vegetables at the beginning of the cooking, as they will require longer to cook.) The inclusion of small pasta shapes is to give the soup more bulk, but if you prefer a lighter soup, you can omit them.

Heat the extra-virgin olive oil in a large saucepan, add the onion, garlic and pancetta, if using, and sweat, stirring, for 3 minutes. Add all the vegetables, (except the peas and broad beans if using frozen) and mix well. Add the stock and bring to a boil, then half-cover the pan with a lid, lower the heat and simmer gently for 30 minutes (adding the frozen peas and broad beans 10 minutes before the end of the cooking time).

Add the ditalini and cook until the pasta is al dente, following the cooking instructions on the package. Remove from the heat, season to taste and stir in the basil leaves.

Serve immediately in individual bowls, with freshly grated Parmesan over the top, if desired.

Zuppa di borlotti e osso di prosciutto

Borlotti bean and prosciutto soup

SERVES 4

12oz/350g thick chunks of prosciutto, rinsed

2 large carrots, cut into chunks

2 onions, cut into chunks

2 celery stalks, cut into chunks

3 tomatoes, cut into chunks

2 bay leaves

a handful of fresh parsley, roughly chopped

20 black peppercorns

14oz/400g borlotti beans, cooked, drained
and rinsed

2oz/55g Parmesan, grated

extra-virgin olive oil, to drizzle

4 slices of country bread, grilled, to serve

In Italy no part of the pig is wasted and it is common to use even the prosciutto bone for soups and stews. The taste is really something else. If I can't get hold of a prosciutto bone, I use thick chunks of prosciutto (which you can ask for at delis) or a piece of gammon (ham). It is a delicious winter warmer and the slightly smoky smell of the prosciutto while cooking takes me back to family evening meals when I was a child. Nowadays, everything fatty seems to be prohibited, but when you make this dish, do include a little of the prosciutto fat – it will really enhance the flavor. If you are using dried borlotti beans, remember to soak them overnight and follow the cooking instructions on the package. Alternatively, if you are in a hurry, the canned variety will suffice.

Put the prosciutto chunks, all the vegetables, the bay leaves, parsley, peppercorns and 2 liters/$3^1/_2$ pints/2 quarts water into a large pot. Place on a high heat and bring to a boil, then reduce the heat to medium, half-cover with a lid and cook for $1^1/_2$ hours.

Add the borlotti beans and continue to cook for 10 minutes. Preheat the grill (broiler) to medium.

Remove the soup from the heat and divide it between 4 heatproof bowls, then sprinkle 1 tbsp of grated Parmesan on top of each. Place under the grill for a minute, until the cheese has melted slightly. Drizzle with extra-virgin olive oil and serve immediately with country bread.

Zuppa di orzo e spinaci

Pearl barley and spinach soup

--- -- --------- --- ----- ---·-

SERVES 4

7oz/200g pearl barley
4 tbsp extra-virgin olive oil, plus extra to drizzle
2$\frac{1}{4}$oz /60g bacon, roughly chopped
2 large potatoes, peeled and cut into chunks
1 garlic clove, peeled and left whole
4 cherry tomatoes, quartered
2 quarts/2 liters hot vegetable stock
7oz/200g spinach
freshly ground black pepper
Parmesan shavings, to serve

--- ----------- --- ----- ---·-

Pearl barley is typically used in soups in northern Italy. When I was growing up we used to have a drink known as orzata, which was made with this grain, but it was on a trip to Scotland during my early years in the UK that I came across it in soup. I have since added it to soups as an alternative to pasta or rice. With the addition of spinach, this is a nutritious and filling meal, which is especially welcome during the colder months.

Rinse the pearl barley in cold water and set aside.

Heat the extra-virgin olive oil in a large saucepan, add the bacon, potatoes, garlic and tomatoes and sauté on a medium heat for 1 minute. Add the hot stock and bring to a boil, then reduce the heat to medium-low and simmer for 10 minutes.

Add the pearl barley, half-cover the pan with a lid and cook on a low heat for 1$\frac{1}{2}$ hours, until tender (check the instructions on the package as they may vary). About 5 minutes before the end of the cooking time, add the spinach. Remove from the heat, season with black pepper and serve sprinkled with Parmesan shavings and a drizzle of olive oil.

SERVES 4

2lb 4oz/1kg beef brisket

2 large onions, cut into chunks

2 celery stalks with leaves, cut into
big chunks

2 large carrots, cut into big chunks

6 bay leaves

20 black peppercorns

a pinch of salt

7oz/200g pastina

Parmesan, grated, to serve

Pastina in brodo di carne

Beef broth with pastina

Pastina in brodo is comfort food and made by mothers all over Italy. It is light, warming and nourishing, suitable for young children, the elderly and convalescents. I suggest making extra broth to freeze in batches. There are many varieties of *pastina* – conchigliette (small shells), stelline (little stars), farfalline (small butterflies), pepe (peppercorns), alfabeto (alphabet) and tubettini (small tubes). My children have grown up on *pastina in brodo* and they love it; even the older ones still ask for it.

Place the beef, onions, celery, carrots, bay leaf, peppercorns and salt in a large pot with 2^1/$_2$ quarts/2.5 liters water and bring to the boil. Lower the heat, cover with a lid and simmer gently for 2–3 hours, until the meat is tender and falls apart. Skim off the fat, if necessary, during cooking.

Remove the meat and vegetables and set aside. Strain the liquid and pour back into the pan, then bring to a boil, add the *pastina* and cook as directed on the package.

Remove from the heat and serve in individual bowls with grated Parmesan on top. You can serve the meat and vegetables as a main course if you wish.

Zuppa di pesce di zia Maria

Aunt Maria's fish soup

- - - - - - - - - - - - - - - - -

SERVES 4

1lb 2oz/500g clams, left in salty cold water
for 1 hour, then any open clams or broken
shells discarded

1lb 2oz/500g mussels, scrubbed and wispy
beards pulled off and any open mussels
or broken shells discarded

5 tbsp extra-virgin olive oil, plus extra
to drizzle

2 garlic cloves, finely chopped

$1/2$ red chilli (chile), finely chopped

9oz/250g baby octopuses (thawed if frozen),
cleaned and left whole

9oz/250g squid (calamari) (thawed
if frozen), cleaned and sliced, head left whole

scant 1 cup/200ml/7fl oz dry white wine

16oz/400g can cherry tomatoes

salt

8 king prawns (jumbo shrimp), shell on if you like

2 handfuls of fresh parsley, roughly chopped

7oz/200g fish fillets such as striped bass,
bluefish, or amberjack

4 slices of country bread, grilled and rubbed
with garlic, to serve

- - - - - - - - - - - - - - - - -

I would like to recreate my Zia Maria's family fish soup, but my version of it has fewer ingredients than she used. Our family loves fish soup and Zia Maria makes the best. When I was a boy we knew the fishermen well and would end up with all the fish they were unable to sell. I remember this soup bubbling away in the large pot, the aroma wafting through the village. This was always a feast and I would rush home to watch my aunt cook and sometimes help with shelling the mussels and clams. Suddenly all the family would reunite in the kitchen, including our pet dog and cat, all anticipating lunch.

Place the clams in a saucepan, cover with a lid and cook over high heat for about 3 minutes, or until the shells have opened. Do the same with the mussels. Discard any clams or mussels whose shells remain closed. Scoop out and reserve the flesh of about half the clams and mussels and discard the shells. Keep the remainder in their shells and set aside. Reserve the cooking liquid from both the clams and mussels.

Heat the extra-virgin olive oil in a large saucepan, add the garlic and chilli and sweat for 1 minute. Add the octopuses and squid and stir-fry for a minute or so, then add the wine and allow to evaporate. Add the tomatoes and salt to taste, then reduce the heat to medium, cover with a lid and cook for 20 minutes.

Add the prawns and half the parsley and continue to cook for 10 minutes. Add the reserved liquid from the mussels and clams and continue to cook for 5 minutes. Using a wooden spoon, make some room at the bottom of the pan and put in the fish fillets. Leave to cook for a couple of minutes, then add the cooked clam and mussel flesh and shellfish and continue to cook for a further 3 minutes, until all of the flavors have infused and the fish is cooked.

Remove from the heat, sprinkle with the remaining parsley and serve with slices of toasted country bread and a drizzle of extra-virgin olive oil.

SERVES 4

4 tbsp extra-virgin olive oil, plus extra
to drizzle

1 small onion, roughly chopped

1lb 5oz/600g zucchini,
thickly sliced

7oz/200g potatoes, peeled and cut
into chunks

3 cups/750ml vegetable stock

freshly ground black pepper

a handful of fresh basil leaves

1oz/30g Parmesan, grated

Zuppa di zucchine e basilico

Zucchini and basil soup

This soup is simple to prepare and light and delicate in taste, with the freshness of zucchini and basil. Liz cooks it when my friend Paolo has a glut of zucchini in his allotment and she usually makes lots to freeze in batches. It is delicious for all the family, and was ideal when my girls were babies. Serve as a starter or with good bread as a light meal.

Heat the extra-virgin olive oil in a medium saucepan, add the onion and zucchini and cook on a medium heat for about 5 minutes. Add the potatoes, stock and some black pepper, increase the heat and bring to a boil. Reduce the heat and simmer gently for 20 minutes.

Remove from the heat and stir in the basil, then blend until smooth. Stir in the Parmesan, heat through if necessary and serve drizzled with extra olive oil.

PASTA

For most Italians a day would not be complete without a helping of pasta. When I was a child, my mother and Zia (Aunt) Maria would make fresh pasta at least once a week. It was usually eggless pasta, which is common in southern Italy, rather than the egg variety that is made in the north. They knew instinctively how much flour and water to use. This was always a happy time, as we children would gather round the long kitchen table to watch them roll out the dough and make different shapes. They chatted while working, and would tell us off for putting our fingers in the dough. They made the pasta by hand (machines were never used) and it was carefully but swiftly and expertly rolled with a rolling pin. They would use long, thin canes and umbrella spokes to make fusilli and ricci shapes and they made gnocchetti and orecchiette too.

We also had dried pasta, as it provided a quick and nutritious meal. But the ritual weekly pasta-making sessions are times I remember fondly and that pasta always tasted more special.

I still enjoy making pasta. I use a machine to roll out the dough and make shapes such as spaghetti and tagliatelle, while the children make nests with ribbons of pasta. I love to watch their faces as they do this — in between the odd argument as to whose turn it is to turn the handle or make the nests! I also make filled pasta, such as ravioli, tortellini, cappellacci, culurzones, panzerotti and mezzelune, by hand and, of course, the girls love to help.

My home village of Minori in southern Italy has a long tradition of pasta-making. Many small factories opened after the Second World War, employing locals to produce excellent dried pasta. I remember pasta hanging on long canes outside, left to dry in the sun, and the short shapes spread out on white sheets on the ground near the sea. The pasta was then packaged in blue recycled paper and sold. As the industry grew, these small factories closed down and were replaced by larger, famous-named factories in town and cities. But there is still a small family-owned shop in Minori run by my friend Antonio, who, together with his family, continues to make his own pasta and sell it to the locals.

Ladies from the older generation in Minori, like my great-aunt Antonietta, still get together, just like my mother and zia Maria did all those years ago, and make pasta. Entire afternoons are spent rolling, shaping, chatting, gossiping and producing great, genuine food. When I return home, I love to visit Zia Antonietta (now aged 90) and her friends and watch and admire. I fear this ritual will die away once these ladies are no longer with us, and that's why I like to show my daughters, in the hope they will keep the tradition alive.

Pasta is comfort food to me – it reminds me of home and I know I am eating a nutritious meal. When I felt a little down as a child, my mother would prepare a quick and simple pasta dish to perk me up and it really did the trick. Over the years, scientists have proved that pasta is highly beneficial in our diet – it's an excellent source of carbohydrates, releasing energy slowly, and contains serotonin, a feel-good substance. Although my mother was not a scientist, she knew what was good for me.

You can make pasta as rich or as light as you like, and to suit your budget. In Italy, the traditional family tends to serve it at lunchtime as a primo (starter), followed by a main course of meat or fish. However, it is perfectly acceptable to serve pasta as a main course with, say, a Bolognese ragù or vegetables, fish or pulses for a nutritious meal.

There are numerous pasta shapes – in the region of 600 – to choose from. When I am in Italy I love visiting the supermarkets to marvel at the varieties, all destined for different sauces and dishes. Italians insist that certain pasta shapes go with certain sauces, and they adhere to quite strict rules and regulations. For example, long pasta, such as spaghetti or bucatini, tends to marry well with quick-cook light sauces such as simple tomato or fish. Short shapes, such as penne and fusilli, go with heavier, more robust sauces such as a meat ragù. This is why Italian households usually dedicate a whole kitchen cupboard just to storing dried pasta. When I visit my sister Carmellina in Italy, the pasta packages tumble out of the cupboard as soon as someone opens it. She keeps a selection of long pasta such as spaghetti (which, incidentally, has varying sizes), tagliatelle, linguine and bucatini; short pasta such as penne, farfalle, fusilli and orecchiette; and tiny shapes for soup such as alphabet or stars, especially for her grandchildren — not forgetting lasagne sheets, cannelloni and paccheri for baked dishes made for special occasions. I like to keep a selection in my cupboard too, and I find a couple of varieties in each category is more than enough for our everyday family consumption.

Pasta fresca

Fresh pasta

- - - - - - - - - - - - - - - - - -

MAKES 300G/10^1/2OZ

1^1/3 cups/200g '00' flour, plus extra to dust
2 eggs

- - - - - - - - - - - - - - - - - -

Fresh pasta can be made by hand simply with a rolling pin, like my mother, grandmothers and aunts did. However, I find it much easier and less time-consuming to use a pasta machine. They are available from kitchen shops and online. For home use, I suggest the small hand machine, but if you regularly make lots of pasta, then it is worth investing in the next size up. You can get electric machines, which mix the dough for you, but these tend to be costly and are very heavy.

Place the flour on a clean work surface or in a large bowl. Make a well in the middle and break in the eggs. Using a fork or your hands, gradually mix the flour with the eggs until combined. Knead for about 5 minutes to form a smooth, soft dough. Shape into a ball, wrap in plastic wrap and leave for about 30 minutes, or until you are ready to cook.

Divide the pasta dough into 4 portions and roll each one through your pasta machine, starting at the highest setting. Continue to roll the pasta through the machine; as it gets thinner, turn down the settings until you get to number 1 and your pasta dough is almost wafer-thin.

Place the sheet of pasta on a lightly floured surface and use according to your recipe.

Non-egg fresh pasta

You can make pasta without eggs. Simply substitute 125ml/4fl oz/^{1}/2 cup hot (not boiling) water for the eggs and follow the method as above.

SERVES 4

1 tbsp extra-virgin olive oil

2 tbsp/30g butter

1 small onion, finely chopped

1½oz/40g pancetta or bacon, finely chopped

9oz/250g podded fresh or frozen peas

6 fresh mint leaves (optional)

generous ⅔ cup/160ml hot vegetable stock

generous 1 tbsp freshly grated Parmesan, plus extra to serve (optional)

salt

10½oz/300g farfalle

Farfalle con pancetta e piselli

Farfalle pasta with pancetta and peas

This quick and easy recipe is especially favored by my girls. I usually make it with frozen peas, but when in season, fresh peas are ideal – just cook them for a little longer and add a little extra liquid. Farfalle is a butterfly-shaped pasta that will particularly appeal to children.

Gently heat the extra-virgin olive oil and butter together in a frying pan until the butter has melted. Increase the heat to medium, add the onion and pancetta and sweat until the onion has softened and the pancetta is golden. Stir in the peas and mint, if using, then add the hot stock and Parmesan, cover with a lid and cook on a medium heat for 3–4 minutes, until the peas are cooked and the water has been absorbed.

Meanwhile, bring a large saucepan of lightly salted water to a boil and cook the farfalle until al dente, according to the instructions on the package. Drain, add to the sauce and mix well. Serve immediately with an extra sprinkling of Parmesan, if desired.

Orecchiette con zucca e broccoli

Orecchiette pasta with butternut squash and purple sprouting broccoli

- -

SERVES 4

3 tbsp extra-virgin olive oil, plus extra to drizzle

$^1/_2$ red onion, finely chopped

$^1/_2$ garlic clove, finely chopped

3oz/85g pancetta or bacon, finely chopped

1 sprig of fresh thyme

$^1/_2$ red chilli (chile), finely chopped

9oz/250g butternut squash, cut into cubes

salt

10$^1/_2$oz/300g orecchiette

3$^1/_2$oz/100g purple sprouting broccoli, stems trimmed, cut into chunks

1oz /30g Parmesan, grated, plus extra to sprinkle

a pinch of dried chilli (chile) (optional)

- -

Orecchiette, meaning 'little ears', are handmade eggless pasta shapes originating from Puglia and traditionally served with a sauce of broccoli and anchovies. It used to be quite usual to see women in this part of southern Italy sitting outside their homes making this pasta; it is still homemade in many households and my zia Antonietta is a 'professional'. As its popularity has grown, factories have begun producing orecchiette and it is now widely available, even here. I really like this type of pasta; it has quite a bite. This recipe uses butternut squash instead of anchovies, making it an excellent dish for all the family to enjoy. If you like a little heat, add some dried chilli (chile) at the end – it really enhances the squash. I love chilli, but usually just sprinkle it on for my wife Liz and me, and the children have it without.

Heat the extra-virgin olive oil in a large frying pan, add the onion, garlic, pancetta, thyme and the fresh chilli and sauté for a couple of minutes. Add the squash, and salt to taste, then lower the heat, cover the pan and cook for about 20 minutes, until tender. Add a couple of tablespoons of hot water if the pumpkin gets too dry.

Meanwhile, bring a large saucepan of lightly salted water to the boil and cook the orecchiette until al dente, according to the instructions on the package. Drain and set aside.

Cook the broccoli in boiling water for about 5 minutes, until tender, then drain and stir into the cooked squash. Add the drained orecchiette and grated Parmesan and mix well. Serve immediately with a drizzle of extra-virgin olive oil, extra Parmesan and the dried chilli, if desired.

SERVES 4

4 tbsp extra-virgin olive oil

1 garlic clove, squashed but left whole

9oz/250g canned good tuna steak, drained

a handful of fresh parsley, finely chopped

2 x 14oz/400g cans chopped plum tomatoes

salt and freshly ground black pepper

11½oz/325g tripoline

Tripoline con tonno

Tripoline pasta with tuna

Tripoline is a long, ribbon pasta. It has a curly edge so that it can trap more sauce. It was one of my father's favorite types of pasta, and I remember him serving it with the season's first San Marzano tomatoes, which grew near where we lived, and raw garlic. The taste was unforgettable. I haven't recreated his recipe, as it is difficult to find these tomatoes in England. But roughly at the same time as the San Marzano tomato harvest, the tuna were in season. The boats would come into our small beach and this huge fish was on show for all to see. My mother would always buy a fair amount to preserve in oil, so I decided to combine the tripoline with this very simple store cupboard sauce of canned tuna and tomatoes. Quick and simple to prepare, it makes a nutritious meal for the whole family.

Heat the extra-virgin olive oil in a large frying pan over high heat, add the garlic and sauté for 1 minute. Lower the heat to medium, discard the garlic and add the tuna and parsley. Cook for a couple of minutes. Add the tomatoes, salt and pepper and stir well, then cover with a lid and cook on a gentle heat for 20 minutes.

Meanwhile, bring a large saucepan of lightly salted water to a boil and cook the tripoline according to the instructions on the package. Drain, then add to the sauce, mix well and serve.

SERVES 4

4 tbsp extra-virgin olive oil
14oz/400g zucchini, sliced
salt and freshly ground black pepper
11½oz/325g spaghetti
4 egg yolks
⅓ cup/100ml milk
1½oz/40g Parmesan, grated, plus extra
to serve (optional)
a handful of fresh basil leaves, plus a
few to garnish

Spaghetti con zucchine alla carbonara

Spaghetti with zucchini carbonara

This is based on the traditional carbonara recipe from Lazio, but I have replaced the *guanciale* (cured pork) with zucchinis (zucchini) for a lighter version. I like making this dish as a quick, simple and nutritious midweek meal for the family. The addition of egg yolks is a great way of adding protein if the children are fussy eaters (but do not give raw or undercooked eggs to the very young).

Heat the extra-virgin olive oil in a large frying pan, add the zucchini and stir-fry on a high heat until golden and cooked. Remove and drain, discarding the excess oil, then return to the frying pan and set aside.

Meanwhile, bring a large saucepan of lightly salted water to a boil and cook the spaghetti according to the instructions on the package.

Whisk the egg yolks, milk, Parmesan and salt and pepper to taste in a bowl. Pour into the frying pan with the zucchini, and the basil leaves and heat through gently, stirring, until you have a creamy consistency. Remove from the heat.

Strain the spaghetti, reserving a little of the cooking water. Add the pasta to the sauce and mix well, pouring in a little of the cooking water, if necessary, to loosen the sauce. Garnish with a few basil leaves, sprinkle with grated Parmesan, if desired, and then serve immediately.

Culurzones

Sardinian ravioli filled with cheese, potato and fresh mint

- -

MAKES 30

5¹/₂oz/150g potatoes, peeled and cut into chunks

2¹/₄oz/60g Parmesan, grated

2¹/₄oz/60g pecorino, grated

2¹/₄oz/60g ricotta

2 tbsp finely chopped fresh mint leaves

salt and freshly ground black pepper, to taste

for the pasta

1²/₃ cups/250g '00' flour, plus extra to dust

1 egg, beaten

for the sauce

scant ¹/₂ cup/100g butter

8 fresh sage leaves

2 tbsp freshly grated Parmesan

- -

I came across this curious filled pasta many years ago on a visit to Sardinia. The shape intrigues me and can be a bit tricky to master – basically, you seal the dough together by pinching the sides and the result looks similar to a Cornish pasty. There are 9 moves to get it right! When I make fresh pasta at home or at demonstrations, I love to recreate this shape, as it always baffles people. However, if you take it slowly for the first one, it really is quite simple and, once mastered, you will whizz through them and wish you had more pasta to fill. The whole family can get involved and see who can be the quickest.

Apart from the intriguing shape, the filling of 3 types of cheese, mashed potato and fresh mint is quite delicious. Believe me, once you start to eat it, you can't stop – but they are filling, so I recommend serving 5 to 6 per person.

For the pasta, put the flour, a pinch of salt, the egg and $1/3$ cup/100ml water in a bowl and mix well to form a smooth dough. Knead for 10 minutes, wrap in plastic wrap and place in the fridge.

For the filling, bring a saucepan of lightly salted water to a boil, add the potatoes and cook for 15–20 minutes, or until tender. Drain well, then mash. Mix in all the remaining filling ingredients.

Remove the plastic wrap from the pasta and leave to rest at room temperature for 2 minutes. Cut the dough in half and put each piece through a pasta machine, starting at the highest setting. As the pasta gets thinner, turn down the settings until you have long thin sheets $1/8$ inch/3mm thick. Place on a lightly floured work surface and, using a 4-inch/10cm pastry cutter, cut out 30 rounds.

To make the culurzones, take a pasta round in one hand, place a full teaspoon of the filling mixture in the center and gently close in half, then pinch a fold of the dough over from the right and then left side to give a pleated effect (similar to a Cornish pasty). Pinch the top to seal. You will have to work quickly, as the thin pasta tends to dry out.

Bring a large saucepan of lightly salted water to a boil, drop in the culurzones and cook for about 5 minutes, until they rise to the surface and are al dente.

Meanwhile, for the sauce, melt the butter in a large frying pan, then stir in the sage leaves and some of the pasta water. Drain the *culurzones* well, then add them to the butter sauce and mix to coat them well. Sprinkle with Parmesan, remove from the heat and serve immediately.

Cappellacci con zucca

Cappellacci with pumpkin

- - - - - - - - - - - - - - - - - - -

MAKES ABOUT 40 CAPPELLACCI

1 tbsp extra-virgin olive oil

1 sprig of fresh rosemary

6oz/175g pumpkin, cut into cubes

salt and freshly ground black pepper

4$\frac{1}{4}$oz/120g ricotta

4 amaretti biscuits, crushed

1 tsp English mustard

1$\frac{3}{4}$oz/50g Parmesan, grated

for the pasta

400g/scant 3 cups '00' flour, plus
extra to dust

4 eggs

for the sauce

scant $\frac{1}{2}$ cup/100g butter

8 fresh sage leaves

6 tbsp vegetable stock

1$\frac{1}{2}$oz/40g Parmesan, grated,
plus extra to serve (optional)

- - - - - - - - - - - - - - - - - - -

When pumpkins are plentiful I love to make fresh, filled pasta. I normally make *cappellacci*, which translated means 'scruffy hats', because of the shape. The filling originates from northern Italy and is one of those recipes I picked up during my travels throughout the country. The pumpkin adds a lovely sweetness, which is always popular with children and adults alike. Although in Italy this dish would probably be served as a *primo* (starter), I find it is a satisfying main meal.

For the pasta, place the flour on a clean work surface or in a large bowl. Make a well in the middle and break in the eggs. Using a fork or your hands, gradually mix the flour with the eggs until combined. Knead for about 5 minutes to form a smooth, soft dough. Shape into a ball, wrap in plastic wrap and leave for about 30 minutes, or until you are ready.

Meanwhile, make the filling. Heat the extra-virgin olive oil in a frying pan, add the rosemary and stir-fry over medium-high heat for 1 minute. Add the pumpkin and salt to taste and stir-fry for 1 minute. Reduce the heat to low, cover with a lid and cook for 12 minutes, until the pumpkin softens. Remove from the heat and mash, then allow to cool. Stir in the ricotta, Amaretti, mustard, Parmesan and salt and pepper. Set aside.

Divide the pasta into 4 portions and use 1 portion at a time, keeping the others wrapped in plastic wrap. Preferably using a pasta machine (see page 32), roll out the dough thinly to just under $\frac{1}{4}$ inch/5mm thick. Place on a lightly floured work surface and cut into 2 inch/5cm squares. Put 1 tsp of the filling in the center of each square, then fold the pasta over to make a triangle, pressing the sides down firmly to seal (use a little water if it helps). Fold the pointed end over, then bring the 2 opposite corners together around your finger to make a hat shape. Continue like this until you have used all the pasta and filling. Bring a large saucepan of lightly salted water to a boil, then cook the cappellacci for a few minutes, until they rise to the surface.

Meanwhile, for the sauce, melt the butter in a large frying pan, then add the sage leaves, stock and Parmesan. Remove the cooked cappellacci with a slotted spoon and add to the butter sauce, coating the pasta well and taking care not to break it. Serve immediately with more grated Parmesan, if desired.

Pasta e lenticchie

Lentils with pasta

This is a dish my mother used to make when we were young; then my sister taught Liz how to make it and now we have it at least once a week. Simple to prepare, it is one-pot cooking at its best. Lentils are a good source of protein and iron and, combined with the pasta, make an ideal meal. Use small brown lentils, such as the Castelluccio variety, which keep their shape during cooking and don't become mushy like the larger lentils. I have used broken-up spaghetti, or you could use shapes like tubettini or ditalini. In Italy, we often add some sausage or pieces of cured pork to give the dish extra flavor.

Place the lentils, tomatoes, garlic, carrot, half the parsley and all the stock in a large saucepan. Bring to a boil, then lower the heat, half-cover with a lid and simmer gently for 25–30 minutes, until the lentils are tender. About 5 minutes before the end of cooking time, add the extra-virgin olive oil.

Add the hot water and return to a boil, then add the broken spaghetti, lower the heat to medium and simmer until the spaghetti is cooked.

Remove from the heat and stir in the Parmesan. Serve with a drizzle of extra-virgin olive oil and extra Parmesan, if desired.

SERVES 4

14oz/400g can of cannellini beans,
drained and rinsed
9oz/250g cherry tomatoes, quartered
2 tbsp extra-virgin olive oil
salt and freshly ground black pepper
12$\frac{1}{2}$oz/360g conchiglie

for the pesto
2$\frac{1}{2}$oz/70g wild rocket (arugula)
1$\frac{1}{2}$oz/40g Parmesan, grated
$\frac{1}{3}$ cup/100ml extra-virgin
olive oil

Conchiglie al pesto di rucola e fagioli cannellini
Conchiglie with rocket pesto and cannellini beans

This is easy to make and perfect for the warmer spring months, when wild rocket (arugula) is plentiful. I like to enlist the help of the girls to collect this versatile leaf. Of course, supermarkets now stock wild rocket all year round, cleaned and ready to use.

To make the pesto, place the rocket, Parmesan and extra-virgin olive oil in a blender and blend to a fairly smooth sauce. Set aside.

In a bowl, mix together the beans, cherry tomatoes, extra-virgin olive oil and salt and pepper to taste.

Bring a large saucepan of lightly salted water to a boil and cook the conchiglie until al dente, according to the instructions on the package. Drain, place in a large bowl and combine with the pesto, beans and tomatoes. Check for seasoning and, if necessary, add more salt and pepper. Serve immediately or serve cold.

Bucatini alle melanzane

Bucatini with eggplant

- - - - - - - - - - - - - - - -

SERVES 4

$^3/_4$ cup/175ml extra-virgin olive oil

14oz/400g eggplant, cut into
thin strips

2 garlic cloves, finely chopped

$^1/_2$ red chilli (chile), thinly sliced

a pinch of dried oregano

2 x 14oz/400g cans chopped plum tomatoes

a handful of fresh basil leaves, roughly
chopped, plus extra to garnish

8 anchovy fillets in oil, drained

salt and freshly ground black pepper

12oz/350g bucatini

3 tbsp capers

3oz/85g pitted black olives, sliced

- - - - - - - - - - - - - - - -

This southern Italian dish has always been a family favorite and was usually cooked during summer. During this time of year we would be surrounded by eggplants and we would cook them in many dishes, as well as preserve them for our store cupboard. I remember my mother saying the best eggplant is the 'cime di viola', a long, thin, bright purple, seedless variety. When I see them here in the market I always buy them. Last year a friend had a glut of this variety in his garden and gave me some – they had a really special taste. If you come across them during summer, I urge you to try them.

Heat 6 tbsp extra-virgin olive oil in a large frying pan, add the eggplant and stir-fry over medium heat for about 10 minutes, until golden-brown and cooked through. The oil will be absorbed quickly, but don't add more – when the eggplant is cooked the oil will exude from them. Remove, drain on kitchen towel and set aside.

Heat the remaining oil in the frying pan, add the garlic, chilli and oregano and sweat over medium heat for 1 minute. Add the tomatoes and basil and cook for 15 minutes. Add the anchovies and cook for 5 minutes, stirring from time to time.

Meanwhile, bring a large saucepan of lightly salted water to a boil and cook the bucatini until al dente, according to the instructions on the package. Drain and stir into the tomato sauce, then add the cooked eggplant and the capers and olives, toss well and serve immediately with a few fresh basil leaves.

Fusilli con datterini e olive taggiasche

Fusilli with baby vine tomatoes and taggiasca olives

This dish can be eaten warm or made in advance to enjoy cold as a salad – perfect for a family picnic! The kids will love the fusilli shape and, even if they are not keen on olives and onion, they will enjoy picking at the healthy tomatoes. If you can't find baby vine tomatoes, substitute cherry tomatoes. I love the unique taste of Ligurian taggiasca olives, which can be found in good Italian delis; but Kalamata olives make a fine substitute, and are widely available.

Combine the tomatoes, olives, onion, extra-virgin olive oil and some salt and pepper in a large bowl, cover and set aside.

Bring a large saucepan of lightly salted water to a boil and cook the fusilli until al dente, according to the instructions on the package. Drain well and add to the tomato mixture, tossing well. Scatter the basil leaves over and either serve immediately or enjoy cold as a pasta salad. Drizzle with a little extra-virgin olive oil just before serving.

SERVES 4

4 tbsp extra-virgin olive oil

$\frac{1}{2}$ onion, grated

1 small carrot, grated

$\frac{1}{2}$ zucchini, grated

6 fresh basil leaves (optional)

generous 2 cups/500ml passata
(strained tomatoes)

2 tsp vegetable stock powder

salt and freshly ground black pepper

$10\frac{1}{2}$oz/300g penne

Parmesan, grated, to serve (optional)

Penne al pomodoro e verdurine

Penne with tomato and vegetables

This is my wife Liz's recipe, and she has made it for our daughters since they were very young. It's perfect for kids, and the vegetables can be blended into a smooth sauce if they prefer. You can make a lot and freeze it in batches, as we often do, for a quick, nutritious meal when you're pressed for time. Of course, it's delicious for grown-ups too!

Heat the extra-virgin olive oil in a saucepan, add the grated vegetables and sweat over medium heat for 3–4 minutes, until the onion has softened. Stir in the basil leaves, if you like, and the passata and powdered stock. Bring to a simmer, then reduce the heat to low, cover with a lid and cook for 25 minutes. Check for seasoning.

Meanwhile, bring a large saucepan of lightly salted water to a boil and cook the penne until al dente, according to the instructions on the package. Drain, then add to the sauce and mix well. Serve immediately with grated Parmesan, if desired.

For older babies and toddlers

Omit the stock powder. Blend the sauce, once it's cooked, to a smooth purée. If you're doing this, there's no need to grate the vegetables, simply roughly chop, but remember to increase the cooking time for the larger pieces of vegetables.

QUICK
MEALS

It's a shame that some people think a quick meal has to be shop-bought and ready-made, something you pop in the microwave. Of course it's much harder to cook from fresh these days, with most adults working and often facing a long commute home. Even in Italy, the land of the cooking mamma, people don't have time to prepare the two- or three-course meals their mothers used to make. However, ready-meals are expensive, and most contain high levels of fat, salt and sugar. And there is nothing nicer than sitting down to a home-cooked meal, whether it's a lavish affair or simply a bowl of pasta with homemade tomato sauce. It is nutritious, tasty and satisfying for the whole family.

Pasta can be rustled up quickly, but there are other easy dishes that can be made in no time and that add variety to your diet. Risotto is the favorite in our house, and I use whatever ingredients we have: peas, zucchinis (zucchini), carrots, broad (fava) beans, pumpkin; sometimes, if the fridge is bare, I serve it simply with butter and lots of Parmesan. Thinly sliced steak and scaloppine of veal, served with vegetables or salad, are also popular, and take little time to cook on the grill pan.

Chicken is quick to cook too, and if you get little pieces such as thighs, they can be roasted in a hot oven with small potato chunks, seasoned with garlic and rosemary, in less than half an hour; serve with steamed broccoli or green beans and you have a wonderful, nutritious meal with hardly any effort. Frittata is quick to make too, and a great source of protein. I add whatever is at hand, for instance cheese, prosciutto, pancetta, peas, zucchinis and onions. I often make a big frittata and enjoy a slice the next day in a sandwich. Fish is also quick to cook, and one of the nicest ways to prepare it is to steam white fillets and drizzle them with extra-virgin olive oil and lemon juice. Served with boiled baby potatoes, or mash for the kids, and green vegetables, this is a lovely healthy and light meal for everyone.

I believe with a well-stocked store cupboard and fridge, you can serve good, well-balanced, nutritious meals every day with a minimum of time and effort.

Risotto

Risotto is a predominately northern Italian dish, but we still enjoy eating rice in the south, and my mother would make her own version of risotto with lots of vegetables. The difference was in the cooking method – she would never stand by the pot stirring, as you should when making a traditional risotto. She would place rice, vegetables, some olive oil and lots of stock in a pot and let it bubble very gently until the rice was cooked and had absorbed all the liquid. She added olive oil and a little pecorino cheese at the end, but never butter and Parmesan. The result was less creamy than a normal risotto, but still very tasty.

I discovered 'real' risotto when I began working as a chef and travelled to northern Italian regions, where rice is cultivated. Here I learned that a number of types of rice work well in risotto (see page 62), as long as you use just one variety.

Like pasta, risotto in Italy tends to be served as a *primo* (starter) and can be combined with a variety of ingredients. It is often made with saffron (a traditional dish of Lombardy), mushrooms, or one of many vegetables, beans and pulses. It can be made simply, with butter and Parmesan or, for a lavish occasion, with shellfish and truffles.

I enjoy making risotto for the family – it's quick and nutritious and the favorite meal of my daughters Chloe and Olivia. I can guarantee clean plates when we've had risotto and it makes me happy to know they have eaten well. But they also enjoy getting involved and love to help with the stirring.

Risotto

Basic risotto

The first rule of risotto-making is to use the correct Italian rice – arborio, carnaroli or vialone nano. Do not use any other type, as the risotto will not work. Next, use good stock: homemade is ideal, but a good cube or powder will suffice. Your stock can be any type, depending on the ingredients in your risotto; for a basic risotto I use vegetable or chicken. Keep the stock gently simmering on the back burner while you are adding it to the rice, as it must be added hot or the risotto will stop cooking. You may find you will need a little more or less than I have used in this recipe. Keep stirring the risotto or it may stick to the pan, and cook it gently over low heat, making sure that all the liquid has been absorbed before you add the next ladleful. Once the risotto is cooked, the pan must be removed from the heat before you add the butter and Parmesan. If you follow these rules and stir for about 20 minutes, there is no reason why you shouldn't have a perfect risotto.

Put the stock in a saucepan and leave it gently simmering over low heat.

Heat the extra-virgin olive oil in a heavy-based saucepan. Add the onion and sweat over medium heat until softened. Stir in the rice with a wooden spoon and coat each grain with the oil. Add a couple of ladles of hot stock and cook, stirring continuously, until the stock is absorbed. Add more stock and repeat. Continue adding stock, cooking and stirring in this way for about 20 minutes, until the rice is cooked. It should be soft on the outside but al dente on the inside.

Remove from the heat and, with a wooden spoon, beat in the butter and Parmesan until the ingredients are well combined and creamy. In Italy, this is known as *mantecare*. Check for seasoning and, if necessary, add salt and freshly ground black pepper. Serve immediately.

Risotto con carne macinata

Risotto with minced pork and savoy cabbage

This is a lovely way of using minced meat; it blends perfectly with risotto. This dish is a favorite quick and simple midweek meal in our house. I find pork mince very flavorful, but you can use minced beef or a combination of the two.

Put the stock in a saucepan and leave it gently simmering over low heat.

Heat the extra-virgin olive oil in a medium, heavy-based saucepan. Add the onion, celery and carrot and sweat over medium heat until softened. Add the bay leaf and mince, increase the heat to medium-high, and cook until the mince has browned all over. Add the cabbage, lower the heat back to medium and cook, stirring, for 1 minute. Stir in the rice with a wooden spoon and coat each grain with the oil. Add a couple of ladles of hot stock and cook, stirring continuously, until the stock is absorbed. Add more stock and repeat. Continue adding stock, cooking and stirring in this way for about 20 minutes, until the rice is cooked. It should be soft on the outside but al dente on the inside.

Remove from the heat and, with a wooden spoon, beat in the butter and Parmesan until the ingredients are well combined and creamy. Check for seasoning and, if necessary, add salt and freshly ground black pepper. Serve immediately.

Risotto con asparagi, zucchini e piselli

Risotto with asparagus, zucchini and peas

SERVES 4

5 cups/1.2 liters vegetable stock

4 tbsp extra-virgin olive oil

1 small onion, finely chopped

1^3/$_4$/350g cups arborio rice

^{1}/$_2$ cup/125ml dry white wine

1 zucchini, cut into small cubes

8 asparagus stems, finely chopped (discard any hard stems)

3^1/$_2$oz/100g podded fresh or frozen peas

2 tbsp/30g butter

1^1/$_2$oz/40g Parmesan, grated

Pour the stock into a saucepan, bring it to a boil, then reduce the heat to low and leave it gently simmering.

Heat the extra-virgin olive oil in a heavy-based saucepan. Add the onion and sweat over medium heat until softened. Stir in the rice with a wooden spoon and coat each grain with the oil. Add the wine and allow to evaporate, stirring all the time. Stir in the zucchini, asparagus and peas. Add a couple of ladles of hot stock and, stirring continuously, cook until the stock is absorbed. Add more stock and repeat. Continue adding stock, cooking and stirring in this way for about 20 minutes, until the rice is cooked. It should be soft on the outside but al dente on the inside.

Remove from the heat and beat in the butter and Parmesan with a wooden spoon. Leave to rest for 1 minute, then serve.

I dedicate this risotto to my daughters Chloe and Olivia, who love it. I like to make it in late spring when the vegetables are tender and at their best. Out of season, I use frozen peas and substitute other vegetables – perhaps carrots and frozen broad (fava) beans – for the fresh vegetables. It's a quick and simple one-pot meal that the whole family will love.

4 tbsp extra-virgin olive oil

4 thin sirloin steaks, each about
5½oz/150g

1 garlic clove, thinly sliced

4 anchovy fillets in oil, drained

1 tbsp capers

a handful of fresh parsley, finely
chopped

14oz/400g can chopped plum
tomatoes

1 tsp dried oregano

salt and freshly ground black pepper

Bistecche alla pizzaiola

Steak in tomato sauce

This dish was a very popular quick meal in our household when I was a child. The tomato sauce was often served with pasta as a starter and then we would eat the meat afterwards. If you don't want pasta with it, serve it with lots of good bread to mop up the sauce.

Heat the extra-virgin olive oil in a large shallow frying pan and fry the steaks for 1–2 minutes on each side to seal the meat. Remove and set aside.

Add the garlic, anchovies, capers and half the parsley and stir-fry for a couple of minutes. Add the tomatoes and oregano, stirring well, and cook over high heat for 1 minute. Lower the heat, return the steaks to the pan, making sure they are covered with tomato sauce, and cook for 10–15 minutes, depending on the thickness of the meat. Check for seasoning and, if necessary, add salt and pepper. Remove from the heat, sprinkle on the remaining parsley and serve immediately.

SERVES 4

4 veal escalopes (scallops), each
about 5^1/$_2$oz/150g

a little plain (all-purpose) flour, to dust

6 tbsp/85g butter

for the sauce

1oz/30g capers, finely chopped

4 anchovy fillets in oil, drained and
finely chopped

scant 4 tbsp/50g softened butter

Scaloppine con salsa di capperi

Veal escalope with a caper sauce

This is a version of the traditional *scaloppine al limone* (with lemon), which is very popular in Italy – the caper paste enhancing the veal. This makes a quick and simple main course for the whole family. You can, if you prefer, substitute pork escalopes (scallops) for the veal. If using pork you may need to increase the cooking time slightly, depending on the thickness.

Mix all the sauce ingredients together to make a paste, then wrap in plastic wrap and set aside in a cool place.

Dust the veal in the flour. Heat the 3 tbsp/85g butter in a large frying pan. Add the veal and fry over medium heat for about 4 minutes on each side, until cooked through. Remove and set aside.

Add the caper mixture to the pan and cook, stirring, over high heat until you have a creamy sauce. Pour over the veal slices and serve immediately.

SERVES 4

2lb 4oz/1kg white fish fillets, such as
cod, hake or plaice

a strip of unwaxed lemon rind

baby potatoes, boiled, to serve

green beans, boiled, to serve

for the dressing

6 tbsp extra-virgin olive oil

juice of 1 large lemon

2 garlic cloves, thinly sliced (optional)

a handful of fresh parsley,
finely chopped

salt

Pesce del pontile

White fish with lemon and olive oil dressing

When I was growing up, fish was abundant and we would eat it often. The local fishermen taught me the tricks of the trade, and we ate the best and freshest produce. This is my favorite way of cooking white fish. Quick and easy to prepare, it is a light but nutritious meal for the whole family, served with boiled or mashed potatoes and green beans. If you prefer, you can omit the garlic.

Rinse the fish under cold running water, then place in a pan with the lemon rind and enough water to cover the fillets. Bring to a boil, then reduce the heat to medium and simmer for 10–15 minutes, or until the fish is cooked through.

Meanwhile, combine all the ingredients for the dressing and beat with a small hand whisk until emulsified.

Carefully drain the fish, place it on a serving dish and pour the dressing over it, then leave it to rest for a couple of minutes. Serve with boiled baby potatoes and green beans.

Sgombri farciti

Filled mackerel

- - - - - - - - - - - - - - - - - - -

SERVES 4

4 mackerel, scaled, gutted and cleaned
1 tbsp plain (all-purpose) flour, to dust
a pinch of fresh oregano
a pinch of fennel seeds
1¼ cups/300ml vegetable oil
lemon wedges, to serve

for the filling

3oz/85g black olives, pitted and finely chopped
2 garlic cloves, finely chopped
1oz/30g capers, finely chopped
4 anchovy fillets in oil, drained and finely chopped
1 tbsp finely chopped fresh parsley
1 tsp finely grated unwaxed lemon zest

- - - - - - - - - - - - - - - - - -

Mackerel is a nutritious fish, and good value too. The mixture for the filling really gives a kick to the fish. Simple to make and quick to cook, this is an ideal, healthy midweek supper for the whole family.

Combine all the filling ingredients in a bowl and use to stuff the cavity of each fish. Secure with raffia or kitchen string, making sure the filling cannot escape.

Combine the flour, oregano and fennel seeds on a plate and dust the mackerel with the mixture. Heat the oil in a large frying pan until a piece of bread dropped in sizzles immediately, add the filled mackerel and cook over high heat for about 4 minutes on each side. Lower the heat, cover with a lid and continue to cook for 3 minutes, until the fish is cooked through. Remove and serve with lemon wedges.

2lb 4oz/1kg chicken thighs and drumsticks
salt and freshly ground black pepper
a little plain (all-purpose) flour, to dust
2/3 cup/150ml extra-virgin olive oil
a bulb of garlic, cloves divided and skins left on
a large handful of fresh rosemary, broken in half
2/3 cup/150ml dry white wine

for the bruschetta
a few slices of bread
a few garlic cloves, peeled

Pollo con aglio e rosmarino servito con bruschetta

Chicken with garlic, rosemary and bruschetta

This is a good old rustic chicken dish, full of flavor, which I love to make when I have friends over for a simple meal. It's easy to prepare, with just a few basic ingredients, and is made in just one large pan. This is exactly how we used to cook it at home at olive oil harvest time. Use good extra-virgin olive oil, as you need quite a lot and the flavor of the dish is really enhanced by it. It's excellent served with the bruschetta.

Season the chicken with salt and pepper and dust with all-purpose flour. Put the extra-virgin olive oil in a large heavy-based frying pan and place over medium-high heat. When hot, add the floured chicken and seal well for 1–2 minutes on each side, until golden brown and quite crisp. Reduce the heat to medium-low, add the garlic and rosemary, cover with a lid and cook for 30 minutes, turning the chicken from time to time. Raise the heat to high, remove the lid, add the wine and simmer until it has evaporated. Check the chicken is cooked; the flesh should come away easily from the bone and there should be no sign of pink when you pierce the thickest part. Skim the oil from the top and set aside.

For the bruschetta, grill the bread, then immediately rub them with the garlic and drizzle with a little of the reserved oil. Serve the chicken with the bruschetta.

Polenta concia con gorgonzola

Polenta with gorgonzola

Polenta (cornmeal) is maize flour, and has always been a staple in northern Italy, especially in rural areas. It has become popular all over the country as well as abroad, and is now served in top restaurants.

Traditionally, polenta took about 40 minutes to cook and required constant stirring. Nowadays, you can buy *polenta svelta* (quick polenta), which takes no longer than 5 minutes to cook. When I was a boy, my mother would stir in lots of cheese for extra flavor and nourishment. This recipe is from my wife Liz's family, who come from northern Italy, and it is served with a slice of gorgonzola on top. It's a quick winter warmer for the whole family.

Pour 4 cups/1 liter water into a medium saucepan, add a pinch of salt and bring to a boil. Gradually add the polenta, stirring constantly, until it is combined. Reduce the heat (polenta does tend to bubble quite a bit), and beware of any lumps forming. If they do, just beat very energetically until they are dissolved. Stir the polenta for about 5 minutes, or according to the instructions on the package. Add the butter, Parmesan and fontina and mix well, until combined. Divide the polenta between 4 plates and top each with a slice of the gorgonzola. Serve immediately.

Polpette di ricotta e limone al forno

Baked ricotta and lemon dumplings

These meat-free meatballs are delicious. My mother often made them when we had lots of ricotta, or when meat was forbidden for religious purposes, such as during Lent. She would enhance the flavor with the addition of Amalfi lemon zest. They can be served with a tomato sauce if desired. Quick and easy to make, they are sure to appeal to children.

Preheat the oven to 350°F/180°C/gas mark 4. Lightly grease a baking sheet.

Combine all the remaining ingredients, except the tomato sauce, in a bowl. Shape into small balls roughly the size of walnuts and place on the baking sheet. Bake for 15–20 minutes, until slightly golden.

Reheat the tomato sauce in a saucepan and serve with the meatballs.

Frittata di cipolle e zucchini

Onion and zucchini omelette

SERVES 4

4 tbsp extra-virgin olive oil, plus a little extra if
necessary
2 onions, thinly sliced
1 zucchini, thinly sliced
6 eggs
1¹/₂oz/40g Parmesan, grated
salt and freshly ground black pepper

A simple, nutritious meal, often made as a main course in Italy. We would have an omelette like this for a quick meal or during religious periods when meat was forbidden, such as on Friday or during Lent. It can be served hot or cold – even taken on picnics – or just eaten with bread as a sandwich. In season, you could use the large spring onions (scallions), which give freshness to the omelette.

Heat the extra-virgin olive oil in a frying pan. Add the onions and zucchini and sweat over medium heat until softened.

Meanwhile, beat the eggs, Parmesan and salt and pepper to taste in a bowl. If necessary, add a little more oil to the pan, then pour in the egg mixture. Cook over medium heat for about 5 minutes, until the bottom of the omelette is golden. Turn the omelette over and cook the other side for about 3 minutes, until golden. Remove from the heat, cut into quarters and serve.

2 tbsp extra-virgin olive oil
1 garlic clove, finely chopped
14oz/400g can chopped plum tomatoes
8 fresh basil leaves, roughly torn
salt and freshly ground black pepper

Salsa al pomodoro

Basic tomato sauce

Quick and simple to prepare, this light tomato sauce is indispensable for dressing pasta and gnocchi, and it makes an ideal accompaniment to *Polpette di ricotta* (see page 77). I suggest making lots of it and freezing it in batches – that way you will always have the basis for a quick meal.

Heat the extra-virgin olive oil in a saucepan, add the garlic and sweat for a couple of minutes, taking care not to burn it. Add the tomatoes, basil and some salt and pepper and simmer gently for 20 minutes. Remove from the heat and use according to your recipe.

pasti a Lunga Cottura

SLOW
MEALS

When there is time, perhaps at the weekends or during holidays, I love to cook traditionally. It's good to slow down, know that I am not cooking in a restaurant kitchen or on a photo shoot, and recreate some of the dishes of my childhood. On cold days I cook huge pots of stew. Once the preparation has been done, I get on with other things or relax while the meat and vegetables gently bubble away on the stove and the cooking smells drift through the house. This is usually when one of the girls will notice and try to guess what's for dinner.

I love to eat anything made with beans or pulses – borlotti beans, cannellini beans, broad (fava) beans, peas, chickpeas, or green, red and brown lentils, as well as many others. They remind me of my childhood home in Italy, where they were a regular feature at dinner during the winter. Like my family, I use dried beans and pulses (but I do keep the odd can in my store cupboard for quick meals); I love soaking them in cold water the night before a meal in anticipation of what I might cook the next day, wondering what herbs and other ingredients we have available to flavor them with. Not only are beans and pulses very nutritious, fat-free and a good source of protein, they are also economical and delicious.

The girls love to help out in the kitchen, and we sometimes make gnocchi, fresh pasta or dough for bread and pizza together. They both adore sausages, so I showed them our simple family recipe for homemade sausages (see page 100) and now they want to make it all the time. Baked pasta and Parmigiana dishes are also favorites, and are good ways of using up leftover salami, cheese, tomato sauce and vegetables. They go a long way too – 1 large eggplant is more than enough to feed 4 people in a delicious and nourishing Parmigiana di melanzane. Filled and baked vegetables – (bell) peppers, zucchini, onions or eggplants – are equally good; a mix of cheese, ham or salami and stale bread, or minced meat, will turn these humble vegetables into really filling and nutritious main meals.

Gnocchi

Gnocchi has northern Italian roots, but the south has its own versions. In fact, the speciality of my village of Minori is *ndundari*, a type of gnocchi made with ricotta instead of potatoes. It was traditionally eaten on special feast days, when my mother would lovingly make it for us, coated in a light tomato sauce. I make it at home now and have converted my wife Liz, who would happily eat it every day.

The most common gnocchi is made with potatoes and, judging by how many packages are sold in supermarkets, like pasta, it is conquering the world.

I prefer to make my own gnocchi, getting the whole family involved in the preparation. The girls love to help – mashing the potatoes, rolling out the dough and cutting it into the small shapes. Gnocchi are simple to make and a great thing to do with the family on a wet weekend. The ingredients of potatoes, flour and eggs are economical and pantry basics, and it's not only fun to make, but the result is so much softer and tastier than the shop-bought variety. I think the experience makes you appreciate good food more and brings you closer together as a family. Children like gnocchi, and its soft texture makes it ideal for toddlers.

You can make variations of gnocchi – for instance, adding chestnut flour to give a slightly sweet flavor (which I love because I'm crazy about chestnuts). Pumpkin gnocchi is popular in northern Italy, and is made using mashed pumpkin instead of potatoes. *Gnocchi alla Romana* is made with semolina flour and baked. Gnocchi can also be stuffed, perhaps with mushrooms or vegetables, but it will be extremely filling.

Whichever gnocchi you prefer, it is substantial and, although in Italy it is served as a *primo* (starter), I like to have it as a single course combined with a light sauce such as pesto or tomato, or simply with butter and Parmesan.

Gnocchi di patate

Potato gnocchi

- - - - - - - - - - - - - - - - - -

SERVES 4–6

2lb 4oz/1kg floury potatoes such as
King Edward or russet, roughly all same
size, scrubbed

salt

1 egg

generous 2 cups/300g plain
(all-purpose) flour

rice flour, to dust

Rice flour is better than plain flour for rolling out gnocchi as it prevents the dough from sticking.

Put the unpeeled potatoes in a saucepan with lots of cold water, bring to a boil and cook for 15–20 minutes, or until they are tender but not falling apart. Drain, allow to cool slightly, then remove the skins. While warm, mash the potatoes and leave to cool.

Place the mashed potatoes in a large bowl, season with salt, stir in the egg, add the flour and work to a soft dough. Sprinkle the rice flour over a work surface and roll out the dough into long sausage shapes. Using a sharp knife, cut into ¾ inch/2cm lengths. Set aside.

Bring a large saucepan of lightly salted water to a boil. Drop the gnocchi into the water in batches and simmer for a minute or so, until they rise to the top. Remove with a slotted spoon and drain well, then add to a sauce of your choice. Mix well and serve.

SERVES 4–6

1 quantity of potato gnocchi (see page 86)

Parmesan, grated, to serve (optional)

for the Bolognese ragù
2 tbsp extra-virgin olive oil

1 small onion, finely chopped

1 small carrot, finely chopped

7oz/200g minced (ground) beef

7oz/200g minced (ground) pork

salt

14oz/400g can chopped plum tomatoes

Gnocchi di patate con ragù Bolognese

Potato gnocchi with Bolognese ragù sauce

This is slow comfort food at its best, a perfect winter warmer for when the children are at home to help make the gnocchi. You can, of course, make the Bolognese ragù in advance – as long as the meat has not been previously frozen, it is an ideal sauce to freeze. Filling, nutritious and fun to prepare, this dish will surely be a winner with the whole family.

For the Bolognese ragù, heat the extra-virgin olive oil in a large saucepan, add the onion and carrot and sweat for a couple of minutes. Add the minced (ground) meats and stir-fry for 3–4 minutes, until browned all over. Season with salt. Add the tomatoes, then fill the empty can with water and pour this into the pan. Lower the heat, cover with a lid and simmer gently for 2 hours, stirring from time to time.

Meanwhile, make and cook the potato gnocchi according to the recipe on page 86.

Add the gnocchi to the Bolognese ragù and mix carefully. Remove from the heat and serve with a sprinkling of grated Parmesan, if desired.

Gnocchi di patate con pesto

Potato gnocchi with pesto sauce

SERVES 4–6

1 quantity of potato gnocchi (see page 86)

for the pesto sauce
2 tbsp pine kernels

1 garlic clove

$1/2$ tsp coarse sea salt

3oz/85g fresh basil leaves

scant 1 cup/200ml good extra-virgin olive oil

2 tbsp freshly grated Parmesan, plus extra to serve

Make and cook the potato gnocchi according to the recipe on page 86.

For the pesto, place the pine kernels, garlic and sea salt in a mortar and grind to a paste with a pestle. Add a few basil leaves and some extra-virgin olive oil, grinding and stirring with the pestle all the time. Repeat until you have used up all the basil and about half the oil and the pesto has a fairly smooth silky consistency. Add the remaining oil and the Parmesan and stir to combine. (Alternatively, you can place all the ingredients in a food processor and blend – although this is not as much fun and you lose the slight crunchiness of the pine kernels.)

Place the gnocchi in a large serving dish or on individual plates. Pour over the pesto and mix well, taking care not to break the gnocchi. Serve immediately, with a sprinkling of grated Parmesan, if desired.

Pesto marries well with gnocchi and the basil sauce really enhances the potato. Children will love to grind the ingredients for the pesto in a pestle and mortar and see them transformed into a silky smooth sauce. This is a lighter way of serving gnocchi, but equally satisfying. Pesto can be made in advance and kept in the fridge for about a week.

SERVES 4–6

1 quantity of potato gnocchi
(see page 86)

for the sauce
scant $^1/_2$/100g cup butter

8 fresh sage leaves

1 tbsp freshly grated Parmesan,
plus extra to serve

Gnocchi con burro e salvia

Gnocchi with a butter and sage sauce

Plain and simple, but totally delicious. The addition of sage gives this a lovely flavor, but if you're cooking it for children, they may prefer just butter and Parmesan, as sage can be a little overpowering.

Make and cook the potato gnocchi according to the recipe on page 86.

Place a large frying pan over medium heat and melt the butter, then add the sage leaves and stir in the Parmesan. Add the gnocchi, with a little of the cooking water.

Sauté for 1 minute, making sure that all the gnocchi are coated in the butter sauce. Serve immediately, with a sprinkling of grated Parmesan, if desired.

Zucchini ripieni al forno con salsa al pomodoro

Baked filled zucchini in tomato sauce

- - - - - - - - - - - - - - - - -

SERVES 4–6

6 large zucchini

2 tbsp extra-virgin olive oil

1 garlic clove, finely chopped

5^1/$_2$oz/150g minced (ground) beef

5^1/$_2$oz/150g minced (ground) pork

3^1/$_2$oz/100g stale white bread, soaked in a little water and squeezed

1 egg

30g/1oz Parmesan, grated, plus extra to sprinkle

a handful of fresh parsley, finely chopped

salt and freshly ground black pepper

for the tomato sauce

2 tbsp extra-virgin olive oil

1 small onion, finely chopped

14oz/400g can chopped plum tomatoes

- - - - - - - - - - - - - - - - -

It is common in Italy to stuff vegetables such as zucchini. Traditionally this is done to enrich vegetables that are in season and make them into a substantial meal for the family. Typical leftovers of cheese, bread and salami are used, while minced (ground) meat and vegetarian fillings are common. This dish is the favorite comfort food of my partner, Liz, whose mom would often make it for her. Liz now makes this for the family and it is indeed yummy and satisfying.

For the sauce, heat the extra-virgin olive oil in a pan, add the onion and sweat over medium heat until softened. Add the tomatoes and season with salt and pepper, then reduce the heat to medium-low, half-cover with a lid and cook for 20 minutes, stirring from time to time.

Preheat the oven to 400°F/200°C/gas mark 6.

Cut the zucchini in half lengthways, scoop out the pulp and put the shells to one side. Heat the extra-virgin olive oil in a frying pan, add the garlic and fry on a medium heat for 1 minute, then add the zucchini pulp and stir-fry for about 4 minutes, until cooked. Leave to cool.

Combine the minced meats, bread, egg, Parmesan, parsley, cooked zucchini pulp, salt and pepper in a bowl – this is best done with your hands. Fill the zucchini shells with the mixture.

Pour the tomato sauce into an ovenproof baking dish. Place the filled zucchini on top, drizzle with a little extra-virgin olive oil and sprinkle with Parmesan, then cover with foil and bake for 35 minutes. Remove the foil and bake for a further 10 minutes, until the zucchini are cooked through. If the tomato sauce has dried during baking, add a little hot water to the bottom of the dish. Remove from the oven, leave to stand for a couple of minutes, then serve.

SERVES 4

1lb 7oz/650g stewing (braising) beef, cut into chunks

salt and freshly ground black pepper

8 tbsp extra-virgin olive oil

a handful of fresh thyme

generous 1 cup/250ml red wine

1 large onion, roughly chopped

2 garlic cloves, crushed

2 celery stalks, roughly chopped

3 carrots, roughly chopped

5$\frac{1}{2}$oz/150g cherry tomatoes, halved

2 bay leaves

5 tbsp passata (strained tomatoes)

generous 1 cup/250ml beef or vegetable stock

Spezzatino di manzo al vino rosso

Red wine beef stew

I love stews and this is one of my favorites, simply cooked with chunks of beef, a few vegetables and red wine. The secret to its rich taste is to cook the beef in the wine before adding the rest of the ingredients, so that the meat absorbs the wine as much as possible. This rich stew, served with runny polenta (cornmeal) or mashed potatoes, is perfect comfort food for the whole family.

Rub the beef all over with salt and pepper. Heat the extra-virgin olive oil in a large saucepan, add the beef and seal over medium–high heat for 1–2 minutes on each side.

Stir in the thyme and cook until all the liquid the beef has exuded (unless you are using aged meat) has evaporated. Add the wine, cover with a lid and cook for 5 minutes. Add all the vegetables and bay leaves and season lightly, then add the passata and stock. Bring to a boil, then reduce the heat to low. Cover and cook for about 1 hour 20 minutes, or until the beef is tender and cooked through.

SERVES 4–6

2lb 4oz/1kg stewing pork, cut into chunks

salt and freshly ground black pepper

a little plain (all-purpose) flour

5 tbsp extra-virgin olive oil

2 onions, thinly sliced

5½oz/150g baby carrots, peeled

1 celery stalk, roughly chopped

3 fresh sage leaves

⅓ cup/100ml dry white wine

generous 3 cups/800ml hot vegetable stock

1lb 2oz/500g waxy potatoes, peeled, cut into chunks

7oz/200g podded fresh or frozen peas

Spezzattino di maiale con patate e piselli

Pork stew with potatoes and peas

This is a simple stew to prepare; however, once you start adding the stock, keep a close eye on it – you don't want to boil the meat. You can substitute stewing lamb for the pork, if you prefer.

Season the pork with salt and pepper and dust with flour. Heat the extra-virgin olive oil in a large saucepan, add the onions, carrots, celery and sage leaves and fry over medium heat, stirring from time to time to prevent the vegetables from burning or sticking, until the onions and celery soften.

Stir in the floured pork and seal for 1–2 minutes on each side. Add the wine and cook until evaporated. Reduce the heat, cover with a lid and cook for 5 minutes. Pour in 2 ladlefuls of hot stock and cook for 45 minutes, adding more stock when necessary.

Stir in the potatoes, with more stock if necessary, cover with a lid and cook for a further 20 minutes. Five minutes before the end of the cooking time, stir in the peas, making sure the potatoes don't break up. Season if necessary and serve.

Cannellini con puntine di maiale

Cannellini beans with spare ribs

- - - - - - - - - - - - - - - - - - - -

SERVES 4

12oz/350g dried cannellini beans, soaked in water overnight

5 tbsp extra-virgin olive oil

1lb 12oz/800g pork spare ribs

4 bay leaves

leaves from 1 fresh rosemary stem

6 fresh sage leaves

salt and freshly ground black pepper

1 onion, finely chopped

1 garlic clove, finely chopped

1lb 2oz/500g passata (strained tomatoes)

a handful of fresh parsley, finely chopped, to garnish (optional)

bruschetta, to serve (see page 75)

- - - - - - - - - - - - - - - - - - -

This rustic dish, traditionally cooked with pigs' trotters and other parts of the pig as well as pieces of lard, was a favorite during winter in most rural regions of Italy. These days, for health reasons, lard and some parts of the pig are not used (except perhaps by traditionalists), and have been replaced by spare ribs, which are equally delicious and less fatty. This dish reminds me of comfort food at home, bringing warmth and cheer to dull, dreary winter days. We would accompany it with bruschetta and the slight charcoaled aroma filled our kitchen and made me ravenous. It was my job to rub the garlic over the bread and drizzle it with the extra-virgin olive oil. Whenever I cook a bean dish such as this one, bruschetta is a must and the smell never ceases to amaze me. It is during dark winter evenings that I love to place dried beans to soak in water in preparation for, and anticipation of, the next day's meal.

Drain the beans, then put them into a large saucepan with enough water to cover – about a scant 2 quarts/1.8 liters. Half-cover with a lid and bring to a boil, then reduce the heat to medium and simmer for 50 minutes, until tender.

Meanwhile, heat the extra-virgin olive oil in a large, shallow pan. Add the ribs, bay leaves, rosemary, sage, salt and pepper and seal the ribs over a medium–high heat for 1–2 minutes on each side. Remove them and set aside. Reduce the heat to medium, add the onion and garlic to the pan and sweat for a couple of minutes. Add the passata, a generous 1 cup/250ml hot water and some salt and simmer for 5 minutes. Return the ribs to the pan and cook over a low heat for about 45 minutes, until the meat begins to become detached from the bone. Remove the ribs again and keep warm.

Drain the cooked beans and add to the tomato sauce, then simmer gently for 5 minutes. Remove from the heat and serve with the spare ribs. Garnish with parsley, if desired, and serve with bruschetta.

Salsicce fatte in casa con salsa piccante

Homemade sausages with a spicy sauce

- -

MAKES ABOUT 10 SAUSAGES, EACH ABOUT 2¼OZ/60G

1lb/450g minced (ground) pork, at room
temperature

¾oz/20g rocket (arugula), finely chopped

1½ tsp salt

scant 3 tbsp/40ml dry white wine, at room
temperature

1 tsp fennel seeds (optional)

1¾oz/50g hard mozzarella, cut into small cubes

5 tbsp extra-virgin olive oil

for the sauce

2 tsp capers, finely chopped

½ red chilli (chile), finely chopped

1 red onion, finely chopped

1 white onion, finely chopped

1 red (bell) pepper, deseeded and
finely chopped

salt

- -

As a little boy I never remember buying sausages from a shop. It was normal for everyone to make their own at home, especially at the time of the killing of the pig, when sausages were in abundance. My sister Adriana and I often make our own sausage, getting the children involved – they love to shape them. I serve them with a spicy sauce; however, for children (unless your's like spicy food) I make a simple tomato sauce. I urge you to buy the best organic minced (ground) pork you can get.

Combine the minced pork, rocket, salt, wine and fennel seeds, if using. Divide into 10 portions. Press a few cubes of mozzarella into the center of each portion, then roll the meat around the cheese and form it into a sausage shape. Ensure the mozzarella is well enclosed.

Heat the extra-virgin olive oil in a large frying pan. Add the sausages and fry to seal on both sides, then cook over gentle heat, turning from time to time, for about 10 minutes. Increase the heat and cook until golden. Remove the sausages and set aside.

To make the sauce, sauté the capers and chilli in the same frying pan for 1 minute. Add the onions and sweat for 1 minute. Stir in the red pepper and add salt to taste. Add generous 1 cup/250ml water and bring to a boil, then lower the heat and simmer for 30 minutes.

Add the sausages and continue to cook for 5 minutes, until the sausages are cooked and heated through. Serve immediately with lots of good bread.

Lenticchie con salsicce

Lentils stewed with sausages

SERVES 4

12oz/350g small brown lentils

4 tbsp extra-virgin olive oil

1 onion, finely chopped

1 bay leaf

2 fresh sage leaves

1 celery stalk, finely chopped

1 large carrot, finely chopped

8 pork sausages

$1\frac{1}{2}$ quarts/1.5 liters vegetable stock

1 large potato, peeled and finely chopped

1 tbsp tomato purée (paste)

When I was a boy, lentils had to be thoroughly checked for impurities and were soaked overnight. These days it is not necessary to do either; however, I always rinse them first in case a small stone is lurking, and for this recipe I usually soak them for a couple of hours – if you don't soak them, you may find you need to cook them for longer. Lentils and sausages are a great combination and this dish is a simple, one-pot winter warmer that is both filling and nutritious. In Italy, for New Year, lentils are cooked in a similar way and served with *cotecchino* or *zampone*, which is a huge pork sausage usually sold in vacuum packs and cooked separately in boiling water. For maximum flavor buy the smaller variety of brown lentils and, of course, good pork sausages from a trusted butcher. This is delicious served with mashed potatoes, especially for kids, or with good country bread.

Wash the lentils, discarding any impurities, and leave to soak in fresh cold water for about 2 hours.

Heat the extra-virgin olive oil in a large saucepan, add the onion, bay leaf, sage, celery and carrot and stir-fry for a couple of minutes. Add the sausages and cook, turning, to seal all over.

Drain the lentils and add to the pan with the vegetable stock and potato. Bring to a boil, lower the heat, cover with a lid and simmer gently for about 35 minutes, until the lentils are tender.

About 10 minutes before the end of cooking time, stir in the tomato purée. Remove the pan from the heat and serve.

Parmigiana di bietole

Swiss chard Parmigiana

- - - - - - - - - - - - - - - - - - - -

SERVES 4

1lb 9oz/700g Swiss chard

$1/2$ tbsp plain (all-purpose) flour, plus extra, to dust

3 eggs

6 tbsp freshly grated Parmesan, plus extra to serve

salt and freshly ground black pepper

olive oil, to fry

$3^{1}/_{2}$oz/100g hard mozzarella, cut into small cubes

a few basil leaves

for the tomato sauce

3 tbsp extra-virgin olive oil

1 small onion, finely chopped

$1^{1}/_{2}$ x 14oz/400g cans chopped plum tomatoes

6 fresh basil leaves

a pinch of salt

- - - - - - - - - - - - - - - - - - - -

Originally, Parmigiana was made with eggplant and although the name suggests it comes from 'Parma', the dish claims to be from Campania and Sicily. I love this dish, which I was literally brought up on, and I also make it with zucchini. Recently my sister Adriana made it with Swiss chard, a spinach-type vegetable that's slightly bitter when raw, but delicious once cooked. It's a shame Swiss chard is not popular in this country, but it can be found at the market during late summer and autumn. When I was a young boy, the Parmigiana would be served as a side dish and it amazes me now how we could eat this along with a starter of pasta *and* a main course! When I make it, it is usually a main course,

served with good bread, to mop up the sauce, and a green salad. Although only the stalks are used for this recipe, don't throw away the green leaves – boil them for a minute or two, then drain and serve with a drizzle of extra-virgin olive oil (you could serve this as an accompaniment to the Parmigiana).

For the tomato sauce, heat the extra-virgin olive oil in a saucepan, add the onion and sweat over medium heat until softened. Reduce the heat to low, then add the tomatoes, basil leaves and salt and simmer for 25 minutes, stirring from time to time. Should the sauce appear dry, add a little hot water.

Preheat the oven to 400°F/200°C/gas mark 6.

You want the white stalks and only the tender inner leaves of the Swiss chard. (The discarded harder green leaves can be used in another recipe or cooked as above.) Wash well and dry, then dust with flour. Beat the eggs, stir in 2 tbsp grated Parmesan, the $1/2$ tbsp flour and a pinch of salt and pepper. Dip the chard in the beaten egg. Pour enough olive oil in a large frying pan to cover the base generously, then place over a medium–high heat. When hot, fry the chard on both sides until golden. Remove and drain on kitchen towel.

Line a 8 x $8^{1}/_{2}$-inch/20 x 22cm ovenproof dish with some of the tomato sauce, then arrange a layer of the chard on top, followed by some of the mozzarella, Parmesan and basil leaves. Continue layering like this until you have used up all the ingredients, finishing with a cheese topping.

Bake for about 35 minutes, until golden brown. Switch off the oven and leave the Parmigiana to settle in the oven for 10 minutes before serving sprinkled with extra grated Parmesan.

Pranzo Domenicale

SUNDAY
LUNCH

I n Italy, Sunday is still considered an important day for religion, family and food. It's the one day when most people don't work and the whole family reunites, usually around the dining table of mamma or nonna. When I was a child, it was the day you wore your 'Sunday best', and I suppose this is still true in smaller towns and villages. I love the atmosphere on Sunday in Italy — the church bells ring and, as Mass ends, the square fills with people, young and old, all immaculately dressed. Some go to the cafés for an aperitivo, some to buy pastries.

When I was a child, my parents, sisters, aunts, uncles and cousins would get together at my grandfather's house for Sunday lunch. He had a big table that would somehow accommodate all of us, up to 25 people. We would all contribute to lunch; my mother brought fresh pasta, my aunt Maria meat ragù, and perhaps one of my sisters a dessert. If my father had been hunting, we'd have rabbit or quail, which he would prepare with my grandfather. It was always noisy, with the children laughing and playing, the dogs and cats waiting under the table for scraps, and the adults discussing the food — where it came from (my father's favorite topic), how a dish was cooked, and arguments about whether it should contain this herb or that. It was fun for me to get together with all my cousins, and now Sunday lunch brings back fond memories of family life in my childhood, and how food was a great part of it.

Sunday lunch might not be as noisy these days, and we might not consume as many courses as we did, but it's good to be together, cook together and share a roast or baked pasta dish. Sometimes my sister Adriana and her sons and my good friend Paolo (who is like one of the family) join us, or perhaps my elder daughter visits with her children, and then it does become noisy!

During the autumn, we often go to the forest to forage for mushrooms. The girls love it, and Olivia can spot a porcino before I do. When we have collected enough, we sometimes enjoy a mushroom risotto in the open; it's a special way of spending Sunday — with family, food and nature.

5 tbsp extra-virgin olive oil

1 small onion, finely chopped

2 bay leaves

1lb 2oz/500g beef topside (top round), cut
into medium chunks

1lb 2oz/500g pork spare ribs

7oz/200g Italian pork sausages

2 tbsp tomato purée (paste) diluted in
1/3 cup/100ml red wine

3 x14oz/400g cans chopped
plum tomatoes

salt and freshly ground black pepper

a handful of fresh basil leaves

1oz/30g Parmesan, grated

Il ragù di famiglia

My family's meat ragù

This has to be my favorite dish and is reminiscent of my childhood Sunday lunches. Traditionally, meat ragù was slow-cooked in terracotta pots for up to 12 hours. It may seem absurd, but believe me the taste was amazing. My aunt Maria was the queen of ragù in our family and each week she would meticulously begin to prepare it the day before, leaving it to cook very gently until late at night, then recommence on Sunday morning, until all the family reunited at my grandfather's house. The tomato sauce was used to dress the homemade ricci pasta and the meat was served as a main course. This dish is still popular for Sunday lunch in most southern Italian families and I certainly like to make it when all the family comes to visit. Of course, the cooking time is greatly reduced. My sister Adriana recently gave me a tip to add chopped Parmesan to the sauce for even more flavor.

Heat the extra-virgin olive oil in a saucepan, add the onion and bay leaves and sweat over a medium heat until the onion has softened slightly. Add the beef, ribs and sausages and fry for a few minutes, turning, to brown well.

Stir in the diluted tomato purée and allow to evaporate slightly. Add the tomatoes, salt, pepper, basil and Parmesan and stir well. Bring to a boil, then reduce the heat to low, cover with a lid and cook for 2 hours, checking and stirring from time to time.

Remove from the heat and serve as suggested in the introduction, with pasta or on its own with lots of good bread to mop up the tomato sauce.

Carre' d'agnello con carciofini

Rack of lamb with artichokes and slow-roasted tomatoes

SERVES 4

4 large spring onions (scallions)
2lb 4oz/1kg rack of lamb
salt and freshly ground black pepper
3oz/85g prosciutto, roughly sliced
1/3 cup/100ml extra-virgin olive oil
leaves from 2 sprigs of fresh thyme
9oz/250g preserved artichoke hearts
9oz/250g slow-roasted tomatoes

This is a different way of cooking a roast rack of lamb – the flavors of the prosciutto, preserved artichokes and sundried tomatoes really enhance the meat. It is simple to prepare and perfect to impress the family on a Sunday

Preheat the oven to 400°F/200°C/gas mark 6.

Cut the white parts off most of the spring onions and thinly slice them. Cut the remaining whole spring onions and green parts in half or into long slices, depending on their thickness.

Rub the rack of lamb all over with salt and pepper. Place the strips of prosciutto between the bones followed by the long spring onion slices and halves. Place in a roasting pan and drizzle with 4 tbsp extra-virgin olive oil, rubbing it well in all over. Place in the oven for 30–40 minutes, or until cooked through.

Meanwhile, heat the remaining olive oil in a small pan, add the sliced white parts of the spring onions and sweat for a couple of minutes over medium heat. Add the thyme, artichokes and tomatoes and cook for a further 2 minutes. About 10 minutes before the lamb is ready, add the vegetables to the roasting pan and return to the oven to finish cooking.

Lasagne agli asparagi

Lasagne with asparagus

- - - - - - - - - - - - - - - -

SERVES 6

2lb 4oz/1kg asparagus, trimmed
butter, to grease
10^1/$_2$oz/300g dried lasagne sheets
(about 15 sheets)
3^1/$_2$oz/100g cooked ham, roughly chopped
2^1/$_4$oz/60g Parmesan, grated

for the white sauce
4 tbsp/60g butter
4 tbsp/60g plain (all-purpose) flour
generous 3 cups/800ml milk
salt and freshly ground black pepper
2 tsp freshly grated Parmesan

- - - - - - - - - - - - - - -

The traditional lasagne that is known all over the world comes from Emilia Romagna, where it is commonly eaten for Sunday lunch. The rest of Italy also has its adaptations. This is a contemporary version made with fresh, light ingredients, and is ideal for spring, when asparagus is in season. I make it for my daughter Olivia – she loves asparagus. It can be served as a *primo* (first course), as Italians would, or as a main course, depending on how hungry you are.

Remove the tip from each asparagus stalk and chop the stalks. Bring a large saucepan of lightly salted water to a boil. Add the stalks and tips and cook for 5 minutes, until tender but not overcooked. Drain, then put the tips on a flat plate. Put the stalks in a blender and liquidize. Set both aside.

To make the white sauce, melt the butter in a saucepan, stir in the flour and, using a hand whisk, whisk to a smooth paste, then add a little of the milk and stir. Gradually add the remaining milk, stirring all the time, until it begins to thicken to a creamy consistency. Remove from the heat, add salt, pepper, Parmesan and the liquidized asparagus stalks, and mix well.

Preheat the oven to 400°F/200°C/gas mark 6. Lightly grease an 11 x 8^1/$_2$-inch/28 x 22cm ovenproof dish with butter. Spread a little of the asparagus sauce on the bottom of the dish. Arrange a layer of lasagne sheets on top, followed by some more sauce, then a layer of asparagus tips. Scatter on some of the ham, then sprinkle on some of the Parmesan and a little pepper. Continue layering like this until you have used up all the ingredients, ending with the asparagus sauce topped with Parmesan.

Cover with foil and bake for about 35 minutes, until golden. Ten minutes before the end of the cooking time, remove the foil.

Coniglio all'agrodolce

Marinated rabbit with olives, capers and pine kernels

SERVES 4

2lb 11oz/1.2kg rabbit chunks, washed under cold running water and dried

plain (all-purpose) flour, to dust

6 tbsp extra-virgin olive oil

1 onion, thinly sliced

5oz/140g bacon, finely chopped

4 bay leaves

1 celery heart, thinly sliced

1³/₄oz/50g raisins, soaked in a little warm water and drained

2 tbsp capers

2 tbsp pine kernels

3oz/85g pitted green olives

3 tbsp red wine vinegar

1 tsp caster (superfine) sugar

salt and freshly ground black pepper

for the marinade

scant 1 cup/200ml red wine

1 onion, thinly sliced

2 bay leaves

20 black peppercorns

Rabbit was always a popular choice for Sunday lunch at home in Italy. My father and grandfather used to hunt and, along with game birds, they would bring home rabbits. My father insisted on cooking what he hunted and my mother was not allowed to do the cleaning and preparing (to be honest, she was pleased). This was always quite a lengthy procedure – after the rabbits had been skinned, they would be soaked in a solution of water and lemon for 24 hours to rid them of impurities, then rinsed a few times and dried, ready to be cooked. We would have them simply roasted with lots of garlic and rosemary, but also as agrodolce (sweet and sour) to enhance the taste of the slightly gamey flesh of the rabbit. I still like to cook rabbit in England and my older son, Christopher, has loved it since he was a child, so when he comes to visit I cook it for him. If you can't find rabbit, substitute chicken or guinea fowl and remove the skin before marinating.

Combine all the ingredients for the marinade in a small saucepan, bring to a boil and cook for 1 minute. Remove from the heat and leave to cool. Put the rabbit in a bowl, pour over the marinade, cover and refrigerate for at least 6 hours, or overnight.

Remove the rabbit from the marinade and pat dry on kitchen towel. Dust in flour, then shake off any excess. Heat 4 tbsp extra-virgin olive oil in a large saucepan over medium–high heat, add the rabbit and cook for 1–2 minutes on each side to seal all over. Remove the rabbit and set aside. Reduce the heat to medium and pour the remaining olive oil into the saucepan. Add the onion, bacon and bay leaves and sweat for a couple of minutes. Add the celery, raisins, capers, pine kernels and olives and sweat for a further couple of minutes.

Meanwhile, heat the vinegar and sugar together in a small saucepan until the sugar dissolves. Remove from the heat and set aside. Return the rabbit to the large saucepan and pour the vinegar mixture over it, then add salt and pepper to taste, cover with a lid and cook on a medium–low heat for 5 minutes. Gradually add 1³/₄ cups/400ml hot water (you may need a little more or less) and cook for about 30 minutes, until the rabbit is tender. The result is a dense sauce. Serve immediately with lots of good country bread.

SERVES 4

1 small head of garlic, cloves separated
but unpeeled

5 large fresh sage leaves, finely chopped

leaves from 2 fresh rosemary stems,
finely chopped

a handful of fresh mint, finely chopped

a handful of marjoram leaves, finely chopped

juice of 1 lemon (keep the lemon halves)

scant $^1/_2$ cup/100g butter, softened

salt and freshly ground black pepper

1 x 3lb 5oz/1.5kg chicken

4 carrots, halved lengthways

extra-virgin olive oil, to drizzle

6 tbsp dry white wine

$^3/_4$ cup/175ml vegetable stock

Pollo arrosto con aglio, limone ed erbe

Roast chicken with garlic, lemon and herbs

I love to have a traditional roast chicken for Sunday lunch, and to make it more moist I spread a paste of roasted garlic and herbs over the flesh. In Italy we used to keep chickens. They were free to roam about the yard and my mom would feed them well. In return, their eggs and meat were delicious. I urge you to buy the best organic free-range chicken you can – it really makes a difference. This is great with Adriana's roast potatoes (see page 169).

Preheat the oven to 425°F/220°C/gas mark 7. Place the garlic cloves on a baking sheet and roast for about 15 minutes, until soft. With the help of a tea towel, remove the skins while still warm. Place the softened garlic in a small bowl with the chopped herbs, lemon juice, butter, salt and pepper. Mix well until you obtain a smooth, but not runny, paste.

Starting at the neck end, carefully ease the skin of the chicken away from the breast, taking care not to tear the delicate skin. Using your fingers, spread the paste evenly under the skin all over the breast, then gently pat the skin to even out the paste. Fill the cavity of the chicken with the lemon halves.

Line the bottom of a roasting pan with the carrots, arranging them in 2 lines like a railway track. Place the chicken on top of the carrots – this will prevent the bird from sticking to the pan. Season the chicken with salt and pepper and drizzle with olive oil, rubbing it well all over. Pour in the wine and stock and cover the pan with foil.

Roast for about 1$^1/_2$ hours, removing the foil 20 minutes before the end of cooking time, until the chicken is cooked through. Pierce the thickest part of the flesh with a skewer; if the juices run clear it is cooked, but any sign of pink and it needs longer. Remove from the oven and leave to rest for 10 minutes before carving.

Triglie al prosciutto

Red mullet filled with prosciutto

- -

SERVES 6

6 x 7oz/200g red mullet (or red snapper),
scaled, gutted and cleaned

olive oil, to grease

dried breadcrumbs, to coat

4 fresh sage leaves, finely chopped

2 egg whites

12 slices of prosciutto

for the marinade

juice of 2 lemons

1 tsp finely grated unwaxed lemon zest

4 tbsp extra-virgin olive oil

salt and freshly ground black pepper

- -

The red mullet is a much-favored Mediterranean fish. They were highly prized in ancient Roman times, when they were reared in ponds and treated like pets, and it is said some were even sold for their weight in silver! I remember when the fishmonger had local red mullet for sale, word got around and people would race to be first in line. We used to enjoy them simply fried and they were always a delicious treat, so I had to include a recipe for this wonderfully delicate fish in this book. Although it is simple enough to make, they take a while to prepare, which is why I've kept them for Sunday lunch. Ask your fishmonger to clean and gut them and I leave it to you to decide whether you want to keep the heads intact – I do.

Put the fish in a shallow non-reactive baking dish. Combine all the ingredients for the marinade in a bowl. Pour over the fish, cover and leave for a couple of hours in the fridge.

When ready to cook, preheat the oven to 375°F/190°C/gas mark 5. Lightly grease a baking sheet with olive oil.

Mix the breadcrumbs with the sage and salt and pepper to taste. Gently whisk the egg whites with a fork. Drain the fish from the marinade. Place 2 slices of prosciutto in the cavity of each fish, then press the edges together to close securely. Dip in the egg whites, then coat in the breadcrumbs, pressing well so they stick to the fish.

Carefully put the filled fish on the baking sheet. Pour the marinade in, around the sides of the baking sheet (not over the fish), and bake for 12–15 minutes, or until golden and cooked. Remove from the oven, leave to rest for a couple of minutes, then serve.

Risotto ai funghi

Risotto with mushrooms

- - - - - - - - - - - - - - - - - - - -

SERVES 4

1½ quarts/1.5 liters good
vegetable stock

4 tbsp extra-virgin olive oil

1 small onion, finely chopped

1 celery stalk, finely chopped

scant 2 cups/375g arborio rice

¾ cup/175ml dry white wine

7oz/200g mixed mushrooms, wild or cultivated,
roughly chopped (if you are using cultivated
mushrooms add ¾oz/10g dried porcini,
regenerated in water – keep the water)

50g/4 tbsp butter

1¾oz/50g Parmesan, grated

salt and freshly ground black pepper

- - - - - - - - - - - - - - - - - - -

England has always been a joy for me – but never more so than when I discovered the many forests and woods full of fungi. During autumn I like to go to the woods and forage; they are a haven of peace and where I feel at my best. I have passed my passion on to my children and, whenever we can on the weekends, we go on mushroom hunts, with both girls competing with each other as to who can find the first porcini and who can fill their basket the fastest. Sometimes, as a treat, I bring the camping stove and we end the day with a mushroom feast, making a wonderful risotto. If you don't have wild mushrooms, use cultivated ones plus dried porcini.

Heat the extra-virgin olive oil in a medium, heavy-based saucepan. Add the onion and celery and sweat until softened. Stir in the rice with a wooden spoon and coat each grain with the oil. Add the wine and allow to evaporate. Stir in the mushrooms and regenerated porcini, if using, adding a couple of tablespoons of the water. Add a couple of ladles of hot stock and, stirring continuously, cook until the stock is absorbed. Add more stock and repeat. Continue adding stock in this way, cooking and stirring, for about 20 minutes, until the rice is cooked – it should be soft on the outside but al dente on the inside.

Remove from the heat and, with a wooden spoon, beat in the butter and Parmesan until the risotto has a creamy consistency. Check for seasoning and, if necessary, add some salt and pepper. Leave to rest for 1 minute, then serve.

Zuppa inglese

Italian trifle

This is not an English soup, as the title suggests, but an Italian trifle. I am not sure where this recipe originates from, but it is suggested that the cooks of the Dukes of Este in Ferrara tried to recreate the English trifle after visits to England. The word 'zuppa' (soup) in Italian cooking refers to both sweet and savory dishes. The trifle is traditionally made with vanilla and chocolate crema pasticciera (custard) and alchermes (an aromatic, herb-infused, red-colored liqueur); I have used Marsala, a traditional Sicilian fortified sweet wine, instead. If you can't find savoiardi biscuits, use lady fingers. This recipe can be made the day before you plan to eat and stored in the fridge, and is a lovely family dessert for a Sunday lunch.

Put the milk in a jug, drop in the vanilla pod or lemon zest and leave to infuse. Meanwhile, whisk together the egg yolks and sugar for about 5 minutes, until the sugar has dissolved and the mixture is smooth and creamy. Add the flour and continue to whisk until well combined. Strain the milk through a sieve, then whisk it into the egg mixture. Transfer to a pan and place over low heat, stirring continuously, until it thickens. Pour half the custard into a bowl and add the cocoa powder, then whisk well, until combined. Leave the 2 custards to cool.

Dip the savoiardi biscuits into the Marsala and use to line a serving bowl. Spoon in a layer of vanilla custard, then lay on more savoiardi biscuits, then chocolate custard. Continue layering, finishing with the chocolate custard, until you have used all the ingredients. Place in the fridge until required. Serve.

FESTE

SPECIAL OCCASIONS

talians don't need a special occasion to celebrate; as long as the table is laid and good food is prepared, every meal is a feast. However, certain times are deemed important: Christmas, Easter, birthdays, saints' days (each town and village in Italy has one), first communion and christenings, to name just a few. Preparations begin at least two days in advance, even earlier for Christmas and Easter. My father used to secure the best fish for Christmas Eve or lamb or baby goat for Easter. Our kitchen was buzzing with activity leading up to the festivities, with my mother, grandmother, aunt Maria, sisters and cousins rolling out pasta, stirring pots of ragù, preparing biscuits and making desserts.

On these occasions we ate many courses, and in traditional Italian families today it is still usual to serve an array of antipasto dishes (which would normally be more than enough for one meal), followed by a special pasta dish – in our house, this was normally a pasta al forno (baked pasta), while in northern Italy filled pasta such as ravioli, tortellini or cappellacci might be served. Then the main course would be meat or fish prepared in a special way, with vegetables and salads. To finish the meal, some cheese, fruit and, of course, a dessert or even lots of sweet treats would be served, as is traditional at Christmas.

Not all occasions require so many courses; sometimes just one dish is prepared. For example, for Carnevale (the week before Lent begins), it is usual to make sweet treats such as chiacchere (small fried pastries) or zeppole (doughnuts). These were traditionally made at home, but can now be bought in pasticcierie, and each region has its own way of making them. On the feast day of our village each year, we celebrate the saint (Santa Trofimena) with a plate of ndundari (ricotta dumplings with tomato sauce).

When I was growing up, your onomoastico (name day) counted more than your birthday. On the day of San Gennaro on 19th September I was always made a fuss of and my mother would make me a special cake. Gradually this has changed, and birthdays have taken over from name days, but some families still make birthday cakes at home and celebrate with the family.

SERVES 4

4 slices of Parma ham

4 slices of mortadella

4 slices of capocollo (cured
pork shoulder)

8 slices of Milano salame

9oz/250g buffalo mozzarella, roughly
sliced

a handful of green and black olives

a selection of preserved vegetables
such as (bell) peppers, eggplants,
artichokes, sun-dried tomatoes and
mushrooms

grissini, bruschetta, focaccia and
country bread, to serve

Antipasto tradizionale

Classic antipasto

This classic Italian starter is traditionally served on special occasions such as Christmas. In rural Italy years ago every family had a pig, which was killed each year so that different cuts of cured meat would be available in the larder (pantry). The family also made numerous jars of preserved vegetables and their own cheese. All this produce would be carefully assembled to be enjoyed as an antipasto or starter. Nowadays, all you need is a trip to the supermarket or Italian deli to find these delicacies. Arrange them on big platters in the middle of the table and let everyone help themselves. Make sure you have plenty of good bread and grissini. You can also enhance this course by making some bruschetta (see page 132).

Arrange the meats, mozzarella, olives and preserves on a large platter. Serve with grissini, bruschetta, focaccia and country bread.

Bruschetta caprese

Bruschetta with tomatoes, mozzarella and olives

SERVES 4

4 slices of good country bread
1 large garlic clove, peeled
4 tbsp extra-virgin olive oil
12 cherry tomatoes, quartered
1 ball of buffalo mozzarella, roughly torn
12 pitted black olives
a pinch of dried oregano
salt
8 fresh basil leaves

Bruschetta was always made with leftover bread, which was toasted in the oven, then rubbed with garlic, anointed with olive oil and finished with whatever toppings were in season. We enjoyed this classic Mediterranean version during the summer. Nowadays, of course, bruschetta is eaten all year round and served in restaurants as a starter. I make it at home, especially when I'm barbecuing meat; the toasted bread with the slight smokiness is delicious. I usually serve it as a starter before the meat is cooked, and no sooner is a plate of it put in the center of the table than it magically disappears and I get requests for more. It is ideal for large groups of people at parties; it looks lovely on a big platter and tastes delicious.

Grill the bread, then immediately rub the garlic over one side and drizzle with half the extra-virgin olive oil.

Combine the tomatoes, mozzarella, olives, oregano and salt in a bowl. Divide between the grilled bread, drizzle with the remaining olive oil and top with basil leaves. Serve.

Raviolini in brodo

Small ravioli in broth

SERVES 4–6

1 quantity of beef broth (see page 20)
1 quantity of fresh pasta (see page 32)
plain (all-purpose) flour, to dust
Parmesan, grated, to serve

for the filling

3½oz/100g cold roast beef
1 tbsp fresh thyme leaves, finely chopped
1¼oz/35g Parmesan, grated
salt and freshly ground black pepper, to taste
2 tbsp dry white wine
1 egg

- - - - - - - - - - - - - - - - - - - -

A small, meat-filled pasta in a good homemade broth is traditionally served during Christmas lunch in most households throughout northern Italy. This recipe was given to me by my wife Liz, whose mother, aunt and grandmother would make it for that special occasion. As a little girl, she would often help her mom on Christmas Eve by rolling the pasta and placing dollops of filling on it (as well as tasting them!), and at the end she had to count the raviolini in order to make sure that there were enough for all the family and guests to eat on Christmas Day. These small ravioli are typically served with a broth, but you can make larger ones, which are normally eaten in a butter and sage sauce or with truffle.

Make the beef broth according to the recipe on page 20. Strain the broth and use the meat and vegetables for another meal.

Make the fresh pasta according to the recipe on page 32. Wrap the dough in plastic wrap and place in the fridge until ready to use.

For the filling, place the beef in a food processor and blend until finely chopped. Transfer to a bowl and combine with the rest of the ingredients. Set aside.

Roll out the pasta in a pasta machine until it is wafer thin (see page 32). Place on a work surface lightly dusted with flour and, using a 1-inch/3cm round cutter, cut out circles. Place a little filling on each one, fold in half and press the edges down well with your fingertips to seal.

Place the beef broth in a large saucepan and bring to a boil, then gently drop in the raviolini and cook for about 3 minutes, until al dente. Remove from the heat and serve with the broth, with a sprinkling of freshly grated Parmesan.

Pasta al forno tradizionale

Special baked pasta

- -

SERVES 6

1lb 2oz/500g rigatoni

3¹/₂oz/100g Parmesan, grated,
plus extra to sprinkle

2¹/₂oz/70g salami, sliced and chopped

3 eggs, hard-boiled and quartered

10¹/₂oz/300g mozzarella, cubed

7oz/200g ricotta

for the meatballs

9oz/250g minced (ground) beef

9oz/250g minced (ground) pork

3¹/₂oz/100g stale bread, crusts removed,
softened in a little milk, then drained

1¹/₂oz/40g Parmesan, grated

1 garlic clove, finely chopped

1 egg

salt and freshly ground black pepper

plain (all-purpose) flour, to dust

good vegetable or seed oil, to deep-fry

for the tomato sauce

4 tbsp extra-virgin olive oil

1 onion, finely chopped

3 x 14oz/400g cans chopped plum tomatoes

a handful of fresh basil leaves

- -

This dish was a must for us on special occasions such as Christmas lunch, a wedding or communion feast. *Pasta al forno* is common throughout Italy and each region, village and family has its own version. It would be made the day before the festivities and everyone had their role in the preparation. My aunt Maria made the tomato sauce – she claimed to be the best (now I think back, this was true!), my sister Carmelina was in charge of the meatballs, perhaps with the help of another sister, and my mother would make the fresh pasta (as was usual for a feast). Even if I sometimes didn't know what occasion it was, I knew when my family got together to make *Pasta al forno* that an important celebration was imminent. This takes a little time to prepare, but the result is really worthwhile.

For the meatballs, combine the beef, pork, soaked and drained bread, Parmesan, garlic, egg, salt and pepper in a bowl. Shape into small balls the size of cherries. Dust with flour, then shake off any excess. Heat oil for deep-frying in a pan until a small piece of bread dropped in sizzles, then cook the meatballs, in batches if necessary, until golden. Drain on kitchen towel and set aside.

For the sauce, heat the extra-virgin olive oil in a saucepan, add the onion and sweat over medium heat until softened. Add the tomatoes and basil and season to taste. Bring to a boil, then lower the heat, half-cover the pan and simmer gently for 25 minutes. Five minutes before the end of the cooking time, add the cooked meatballs. When cooked, remove from the heat and, using a slotted spoon, lift out the meatballs and set aside on a plate.

Preheat the oven to 400°F/200°C/gas mark 6.

Cook the rigatoni in lightly salted water until al dente, according to the instructions on the package. Drain and return to the saucepan with half the tomato sauce and half the Parmesan, and stir gently.

Line an ovenproof dish with some of the tomato sauce. Spoon some pasta over the sauce, then a little of the salami, some egg quarters, mozzarella, ricotta, Parmesan and meatballs. Continue layering like this until you have used up all the ingredients, ending with tomato sauce and a sprinkling of Parmesan. Bake for 40 minutes. Leave to rest for a couple of minutes, then serve.

Porchetta

Stuffed rolled pork belly

- -

11lb/5kg pork belly (ask your butcher to remove the ribs and trim the excess fat)

1oz/25g coarse sea salt

freshly ground coarse black pepper

small green leaves from a large handful of fresh thyme

leaves from a large handful of fresh rosemary, roughly chopped

a large handful of fresh sage leaves, roughly chopped

1 tbsp fennel seeds (if you are lucky enough to find wild fennel use it)

8 garlic cloves, finely chopped

2 tbsp extra-virgin olive oil

potatoes, peeled and cut into chunks

small carrots, cut into chunks

6 tbsp honey

- -

Porchetta to me means a party and I make it during special occasions, when I know hordes of people will drop by. It feeds lots, can be eaten cold and can be stored in the fridge for up to a week. Traditionally in Italy, *porchetta* is a whole piglet filled with lots of fresh herbs and slow-roasted either in a wood oven or even outdoors on a spit. It is made at home, as well as sold ready-made as a takeaway. Since whole piglets are not that easily obtainable, I use pork belly and the result is similar. It is simple to prepare and can be made in advance and eaten cold – a great idea for large gatherings. It's ideal served with preserved vegetables such as Giardiniera (see page 224) and Preserved eggplants (see page 226).

Preheat the oven to 425°F/220°C/Gas 7. Lay the pork belly flat, skin side down. Sprinkle with half the salt and lots of black pepper, rubbing it well into the meat with your fingers. Leave to rest for 10 minutes so that the seasoning settles well into the meat. Sprinkle the herbs, fennel seeds and garlic evenly all over.

You will need 10 pieces of string, each about 12 inches/30cm long. Carefully roll the meat up widthways and tie it very tightly with string in the middle of the joint. Then tie at either end about 1/2 inch/1cm from the edge and keep tying along the joint until you have used up all the string. The filling should be well wrapped – if any escapes from the sides, push it in. Using your hands, massage 1 tbsp extra-virgin olive oil over the joint, then rub in the remaining salt and some more black pepper.

Grease a large roasting pan with the remaining olive oil and place the pork in it. Roast for 10 minutes, then turn it over. After 15 minutes, reduce the oven temperature to 300°F/150°C/gas mark 2 and cover the pork with foil (if you like the crackling to be very crispy, don't bother with the foil, but remember the *porchetta* needs to be thinly sliced and crispy crackling will make that difficult). Roast for 3 hours.

If cooking the potatoes and carrots, add them to the roasting dish for the final 1 1/2 hours of cooking.

Remove the joint from the oven and coat with the honey, drizzling some of the juices from the roasting pan over it too. Insert a fork at either side of the joint and lift onto a wooden board. Leave to rest for 5 minutes, then slice and serve hot or cold.

Soffritto Napoletano

Spicy meat stew

SERVES 6–8

1lb 2oz/500g pig's liver

10$\frac{1}{2}$oz/300g pig's lung

10$\frac{1}{2}$oz/300g pig's heart

2 pig's kidneys

$\frac{1}{2}$ pig's spleen

4 tbsp olive oil

7oz/200g pork lard

generous 1 cup/250ml red wine

4 red chillies (chiles), finely chopped

1 red bell pepper, roasted, deseeded and finely chopped

5 bay leaves

1 fresh rosemary sprig

a small handful of fresh sage

6 tbsp tomato purée (paste)

4 cups/1 liter hot vegetable stock

6 large bread rolls, soft crumb pulled out and discarded, or thick slices of rustic bread, oven-baked on a low setting until crispy

extra-virgin olive oil, to drizzle

This is not an obvious recipe for a family book, but in my family it was very popular, especially among the men. When I was a boy, the local inns in the village would serve it as a working man's breakfast, presented in a large hollow bread roll, which certainly kept the men going for most of the day. This 400-year-old Neapolitan recipe originates from *cucina povera*, when the poor would wait outside the kitchens of the rich nobles for the discarded innards of the beasts being cooked. They took the innards home to their wives, who came up with this spicy recipe. Many would say that this poor man's dish – *soffritto* – actually tasted better than the rich man's meal.

Wash the liver, lung, heart, kidneys and spleen in cold water and dry them with a cloth, then slice them into small chunks.

Heat the olive oil and lard in a large saucepan. Add the liver, lung, heart, kidneys and spleen and cook, stirring, until everything is well sealed on all sides. Add the wine and allow to evaporate, then stir in the chillies, roasted pepper, bay leaves, rosemary, sage and tomato purée and cook for 5 minutes. Add the hot stock and simmer for about 1 hour, checking from time to time to ensure that the meat isn't sticking, and if necessary adding some more stock. At the end of the cooking time, the stew should have a creamy consistency.

Place the crispy bread rolls or slices on individual plates, fill with the soffritto, drizzle with extra-virgin olive oil and serve immediately. Alternatively, serve on slices of baked bread.

Agnello brodettato

Easter lamb

SERVES 4

4 tbsp extra-virgin olive oil
2lb 4oz/1kg lamb shoulder, cut into chunks
1 onion, finely chopped
1½oz/40g prosciutto, roughly chopped
¾ cup/175ml dry white wine
2 quarts/2 liters hot vegetable stock
1 potato, peeled and cut into small chunks
yolks from 2 hard-boiled eggs
1 fresh marjoram stalk
1 tbsp finely chopped fresh parsley
finely grated zest and juice of ½ small
unwaxed lemon

This is a traditional dish prepared at Easter in most of central and southern Italy, using the new season's spring baby lamb and eggs. Originally it was made with baby goat and raw eggs, in the days when you knew where your eggs came from (probably your own backyard). When I was a child, my family would always celebrate Easter by cooking a baby goat, and sometimes *brodettato*-style (which roughly translates as 'in a broth'). I have added lemon, herbs and hard-boiled egg yolks for a lighter alternative. The sauce is delicate and tasty. Serve with boiled new potatoes and the new season's fresh peas.

Heat the extra-virgin olive oil in a large saucepan, add the lamb and brown well all over on a high heat. Reduce the heat to medium, add the onion and prosciutto and stir-fry for 3 minutes. Add the wine and allow to evaporate. Add the hot stock and potato, cover with a lid and cook for 45 minutes, until the lamb is cooked and tender.

Remove the lamb and set aside. Remove the sauce from the heat, stir in the hardboiled egg yolks, herbs and lemon juice and liquidize to a smooth, creamy sauce. Serve immediately with the lamb chunks and a sprinkling of lemon zest.

Fritto misto di pesce

Mixed fried fish

SERVES 4

7oz/200g king prawns (jumbo shrimp),
raw and unpeeled

7oz/200g whitebait

7oz/200g squid (calamari), cleaned
and cut into rings and tentacles

7oz/200g sardines, gutted

grated zest of 2 unwaxed lemons

1 small garlic clove, finely chopped

a handful of fresh parsley, finely chopped

good vegetable or seed oil, to deep-fry

lemon wedges, to serve

for the batter

2 egg yolks

a pinch of salt

1 1/3 cups/200g plain
(all-purpose) flour, sifted

This dish was commonly served during the Christmas Eve feast, when meat was not permitted and the meal consisted of fish and vegetables. A large platter of *fritto misto* was placed in the middle of the table and everyone helped themselves. *Fritto misto* is also popular in restaurants at coastal resorts throughout Italy. The traditional way of making this dish was to simply dust the fish with flour and then fry them. I like a light batter, which works really well with the delicate flavor of the fish. The secret of this recipe is to use really fresh fish.

Place the prawns, whitebait, squid and sardines in a shallow dish and scatter half the lemon zest and all the garlic and parsley over them. Cover and refrigerate for 30 minutes.

To make the batter, whisk the egg yolks in a bowl, then gradually whisk in a scant 3 tbsp/40ml very cold water and the salt. Gradually fold in the flour, until well combined.

Heat the oil for deep-frying in a large saucepan or deep-fryer until a small piece of bread dropped in sizzles immediately. Remove the fish from the fridge and dip each piece into the batter, then immediately fry a few pieces at a time for a few minutes, until golden and the fish is cooked. Drain on kitchen towel and serve immediately, scattered with the remaining lemon zest, with lemon wedges.

Spiedini di polipo

Skewered octopus

- - - - - - - - - - - - - - - - - -

MAKES ABOUT 10 SKEWERS

2lb 4oz/1kg octopus (thawed if frozen)

4 bay leaves

1 fresh rosemary sprig

½ tbsp black peppercorns

2 slices of unwaxed lemon zest

olive oil, to grease

5½oz/150g breadcrumbs (pulse stale crustless rustic bread in a food processor)

a handful of fresh parsley, finely chopped

1 fresh thyme sprig, finely chopped

1 fresh marjoram sprig, finely chopped

1 garlic clove, finely chopped

1 large red onion, thickly sliced

salt and freshly ground black pepper

- - - - - - - - - - - - - - - - - -

Octopus reminds me of my youth, diving deep down into the sea to collect these amazing sea creatures. The ones I collected lived by the rocks and were slightly grey and smaller than normal, weighing no more than about 14oz/400g each. These smaller ones can be simply cooked with a little extra-virgin olive oil in their own juice. The larger ones were found out in the ocean and were caught by fishermen using *luce dei lampari* (oil lamps), which were lit at night to attract the octopus, which would come up to the surface to investigate. The larger octopus has to be cooked in water with some herbs, as in this recipe. These skewers make a great alternative to the usual meat ones and, with the red onion and herby breadcrumbs, are really delicious. They take a little time to prepare, but are well worth the effort when friends come round. They can be served as an antipasto or as part of a selection of dishes at a party. If you have any breadcrumbs left over, put them on a baking tray and bake for a few minutes until golden. Use them to top the skewers just before serving.

Bring a large saucepan of water to a boil. Pick the octopus up by its head and gently dip into the boiling water 3 times. You will notice the tentacles curl up. Discard the boiling water.

Place the octopus in a large clean saucepan with the bay leaves, rosemary, peppercorns and lemon zest and fill with cold water. Bring to a boil, then reduce the heat, partially cover with a lid and simmer gently for 50 minutes or until the octopus is tender. Remove from the heat and leave the octopus in the cooking water to settle for about 30 minutes. Preheat the oven to 375°F/190°C/gas mark 5. Lightly grease a baking tray (sheet) with extra-virgin olive oil.

Meanwhile, mix together the breadcrumbs, herbs and garlic in a bowl. Remove the octopus from the pan and drain, then slice into chunks. Thread alternate chunks of octopus and onion slices on to the skewers. Coat the skewers in the breadcrumb mixture. Place on the baking tray, drizzle with some extra-virgin olive oil and sprinkle with salt and pepper.

Bake for 5 minutes, then turn the skewers over, add some of the leftover breadcrumb mixture and continue baking until golden. Can be enjoyed warm or cold.

Torta festiva

Celebration cake

butter, to grease
6 eggs
1 1/2 cups/300g caster (superfine) sugar
1 1/3 cups/200g plain (all-purpose)
flour, sifted
3 tsp baking powder, sifted

for the filling
3 cups/750ml milk
1 vanilla pod
9 egg yolks
1 1/2 cups/300g caster (superfine) sugar
2 3/4 oz/75g cornflour (cornstarch)
2 1/4 oz/60g good plain (semisweet)
chocolate, finely chopped

for the syrup
1/3 cup/100ml Marsala
scant 1/4 cup/40g caster
(superfine) sugar

for the decoration
a selection of fruit, such as strawberries, kiwi,
blueberries, cherries, raspberries and figs
icing (confectioners') sugar, sifted

This is a typical Italian celebration cake, made for birthdays and other festivities. The sponge, known as *pan di spagna*, is drizzled with a syrup made from water and a sweet liqueur, which makes it very moist. The filling is usually a *crema pasticciera* (custard cream), which is homemade and can be flavored with vanilla and/or chocolate.

This cake can be decorated as you like; I use fresh fruit, which is quite traditional. However, you can use your imagination and make a cake that is suitable for any member of your family, for any occasion. My sister Adriana is an expert cake maker and decorator and makes this cake for her sons' birthdays, changing the decorations accordingly.

First, make the sponge. Preheat the oven to 350°F/180°C/ gas mark 4. Grease a deep 8-inch/20cm square cake pan, or 3 x 8-inch/20cm round sandwich pans if you have them, then set aside.

For the sponge, whisk the eggs and sugar together in a bowl until creamy and foamy. Gradually fold in the flour and baking powder. Pour into the cake pan/s and bake for 40 minutes if using a large pan and 15–20 minutes if using small pans.

CONTINUED OVERLEAF...

Check it is done by inserting a wooden skewer, if it comes out clean and dry the sponge is ready. Leave to cool, then tip out of the tin/s. If you have made 1 cake, cut it horizontally into 3 sponges.

For the filling, pour the milk into a small saucepan, add the vanilla pod and heat until the milk reaches boiling point. Meanwhile, whisk the egg yolks and sugar in a bowl until light and fluffy. Add the cornflour and continue to whisk.

Gradually pour the milk into the egg mixture, whisking all the time to prevent lumps forming. Once well combined, pour the mixture back into the pan, place over medium heat and stir. As soon as it begins to boil, remove from the heat (do this quickly or the cream on the bottom of the pan will burn).

Pour a third of the mixture into another bowl and immediately stir in the chocolate until well combined and the chocolate has melted. You will then have a vanilla filling and a chocolate filling – cover both with plastic wrap and leave to cool.

For the syrup, put the Marsala and sugar in a small saucepan with a scant 1 cup/200ml water and cook on a medium heat, stirring, until the sugar has dissolved and the liquid has reduced a little. Leave to cool. Brush each layer of sponge with the syrup.

Spread the first sponge layer with vanilla filling. Add a second layer of sponge and spread with the chocolate filling. Add a third layer of sponge and top with the remaining vanilla filling. Decorate with the fruit and dust with sifted icing sugar.

Chiacchiere

Carnival biscuits

- -

SERVES 4–6

generous 2 cups/300g plain
(all-purpose) flour
$^1/_3$ cup/70g caster (superfine) sugar
2 eggs, beaten
scant $^1/_2$ cup/100g butter, melted
finely grated zest of 1 unwaxed lemon
5 tsp rum
good vegetable oil, to deep-fry
icing (confectioners') sugar, to dust

- -

These are traditional biscuits made all over Italy for *Carnevale*, the period just before Lent, and are known by various regional names. I enjoy making them each year with my girls – we roll out the pastry with the pasta machine and then cut them out with a pasta cutter, giving the biscuits a decorative curly edge. They are light and delicious and once you start eating one, you don't stop, so it's always worth making lots.

Place the flour on a clean work surface and make a well in the center. Add the sugar, eggs, butter, lemon zest and rum and mix well to form a smooth dough. Wrap in plastic wrap and place in the fridge for a couple of hours.

Lightly flour a work surface and roll out the dough in a rectangular shape to a thickness of $^1/_8$ inch/3mm. Using a pastry cutter, cut into strips of $^3/_4$ inch/2cm wide, making a small incision with the cutter in the middle of each strip.

Heat the vegetable oil for deep frying in a large saucepan or deep-fryer until a small piece of bread dropped into it sizzles immediately. Add the chiacchere in batches of a few at a time and fry, turning each one until they are golden brown. Drain on kitchen towel, allow to cool, then sprinkle with some icing sugar.

Frittelle dolci di patate

Potato doughnuts

- - - - - - - - - - - - - - - - - - -

MAKES ABOUT 12

9oz/250g floury potatoes

1²/₃ cups/250g '00' flour or strong plain
(all-purpose bread) flour, plus extra to dust

1 x 7g sachet of dried yeast, dissolved in 2 tbsp
lukewarm water

2 eggs

¹/₄ cup/50g caster (superfine) sugar,
plus extra to dust

scant 4 tbsp/50g butter, softened

a pinch of salt

finely grated zest of 1 orange

1 vanilla pod

good vegetable or seed oil, to fry

cinnamon powder, to dust

- - - - - - - - - - - - - - - - - - -

This sweet doughnut made with potato is a recipe
from the Amalfi coast, where they are made during
Carnevale, when people throw parties and eat lots
of sweet treats. It is a typical recipe from home and
not a dish you'll find in the pastry shops. I remember
as a child helping my older sisters to roll the dough
out and I couldn't wait for them to be cooked and
ready for me to eat. They are lighter and much
healthier than the usual shop-bought versions.

Boil the potatoes in their skins for 15–25 minutes, until
tender. Cool a little, then remove the skins and mash
the potatoes with a ricer.

Place the flour in a large bowl or on a clean work
surface, make a well in the center and add the
mashed potato, dissolved yeast, eggs, sugar, butter,
salt and orange zest. Split the vanilla pod lengthways
and scrape out the seeds, then add them too.
Using your hands, gradually mix all these ingredients
together to form a smooth, elastic dough. Shape into
a ball, wrap in plastic wrap and leave to rest at room
temperature for 30 minutes.

Remove the plastic wrap and divide the dough into
quarters. Roll each piece into a long sausage shape,
about ⁵/₈ inch/15mm thick, and cut into 6 inch/15cm
lengths. Form each length into a circle and seal the
ends. Cover with a cloth and leave in a warm place
for about 30 minutes, until they have doubled in size.

Heat the vegetable oil for deep frying in a large
saucepan or deep-fryer until a small piece of bread
dropped in sizzles immediately. Reduce the heat
to medium and fry the doughnuts, a few at a time,
turning, until golden on all sides. Drain on kitchen
towel. Combine the sugar and cinnamon powder
and coat the doughnuts. Serve warm or cold.

Contorni

ON
THE SIDE

We are lucky in Italy to have a wide variety of vegetables and salad ingredients. For this we must thank all the invaders who came to our country in ancient times, introducing us to delights such as olive trees, vines and citrus fruits, as well as a multitude of greens and even tomatoes. Generally we eat vegetables in season, and when I was young all the produce was local; some came from our garden, and anything bought from market stalls was picked that morning. Most of the herbs came from the hills above the village. Each season brought its specialities: with spring came tender sweet peas and broad (fava) beans, the first baby carrots, zucchini, salad leaves, rocket (arugula), dandelion, spinach and asparagus and much more. As we went into summer, yellow, red, orange and green peppers of all shapes and sizes added color and variety to the plate, as did eggplant and, of course, our beloved tomato. When the days became cooler and shorter and colorful leaves littered the ground, it was time to go foraging for wild mushrooms. Pumpkins took pride of place on market stalls, as did the first root vegetables: beetroot, carrots and potatoes. One of the few signs of life in winter was the pretty, purplish artichoke flowers growing in gardens, brightening up bleak days.

Vegetables played an important part in our diet and were eaten not only as a side dish, but also as a main course. Stuffing peppers, eggplants, onions and zucchini is a great way of making them go further and creating nutritious dishes for the whole family. Vegetables are added to pasta and risotto and make bakes. The humble escarole, a lettuce-type vegetable, was often made into a main meal; I remember my nonna would fill it with all sorts of leftovers — bits of cheese, salami, stale bread, olives, capers — to make a nutritious meal for the whole family.

Most Italians dress their vegetables and for a milder flavor good olive oil and lemon is all that is needed.

SERVES 4

salt and freshly ground black pepper

1lb 9oz/700g escarole, roughly chopped

4 tbsp extra-virgin olive oil

1 large onion, finely chopped

4 thyme sprigs

7oz/200g frozen peas

scant 1 cup/200ml hot vegetable stock

1 garlic clove, left whole

1³⁄₄oz/50g pancetta or bacon, roughly chopped

Scarola e piselli

Escarole and peas

Escarole is popular in southern Italy and is the least bitter of the endive family. It resembles a large lettuce, but the outer leaves are coarser and quite tough, so it is always cooked. Escarole was common during the winter when I was a child, and we would have it often, either braised like this or filled with leftovers, as my nonna would make. I have combined the escarole with peas to make a healthy side dish to accompany meat. If you increase the quantities, it can be eaten on its own, with good bread, as a light meal.

Bring a medium saucepan of lightly salted water to a boil, add the escarole and cook for about 10 minutes, until tender. Drain well and set aside.

Meanwhile, heat 3 tbsp extra-virgin olive oil in a large frying pan, add the onion and thyme and sweat over medium heat for 5 minutes, or until softened. Add the peas, hot stock and a little pepper, cover with a lid and cook for a further 5 minutes.

Heat the remaining olive oil in another frying pan, add the garlic and pancetta and stir-fry over medium–high heat for 5 minutes, or until golden. Add the escarole, some salt and pepper and cook for another 5 minutes. Reduce the heat to medium, add the pea mixture, mix well and cook for a further 5 minutes. Serve.

SERVES 4

9oz/250g asparagus, cleaned and
ends trimmed

salt

1oz/25g blanched almonds, toasted

12 fresh mint leaves

1 tbsp capers

4 tbsp extra-virgin olive oil

Asparagi con pesto alle mandorle

Asparagus with almond pesto

In Italy I would always go out in spring to pick the long, thin wild asparagus. It was not until I came to England that I discovered the larger variety, which is ideal for dipping into sauces like this one. Almond pesto is common in Sicily for dressing pasta, and it marries really well with asparagus. This is an ideal starter or side dish, or to serve at parties.

Bring a medium saucepan of lightly salted water to a boil, add the asparagus and cook for about 5 minutes, until tender. Drain and arrange on a serving plate.

Blend the other ingredients to a fairly smooth consistency in a food processor and serve with the cooked asparagus.

Broccoli con aglio, olio e peperoncino

Sautéed long stem broccoli with garlic and chilli

SERVES 4

4 tbsp extra-virgin olive oil
3 garlic cloves, thinly sliced
1 small red chilli (chile), finely chopped
14oz/400g long stem broccoli, stems trimmed
salt and freshly ground black pepper
juice of ½ lemon (optional)

Broccoli is such a nutritious vegetable and I especially like the long-stem or purple sprouting variety. I love it with lots of chilli (chile) and garlic, but for the children I add less chilli or omit it altogether. This makes a lovely accompaniment to sausages and other meat dishes, or can be enjoyed with bread as a light meal.

Heat the extra-virgin olive oil in a frying pan, add the garlic and chilli and sweat for 1 minute over medium–high heat. Add the broccoli and some salt and pepper and stir-fry for 1 minute. Add ⅔ cup/150ml water, reduce the heat to medium, cover with a lid and cook for about 10 minutes, until tender.

Remove the lid, increase the heat and allow the liquid to evaporate. Remove from the heat, pour in the lemon juice, if using, and serve.

SERVES 4

6 tbsp extra-virgin olive oil

1 yellow bell pepper, deseeded and
cut into strips

1 red bell pepper, deseeded and cut
into strips

3 anchovy fillets in oil, drained (optional)

2 garlic cloves, thinly sliced

10 pitted green olives

1 tbsp capers

1 tbsp caster (superfine) sugar

4 tbsp white wine vinegar

salt and freshly ground black pepper

a small handful of curly parsley, roughly
chopped

Peperoni all'agrodolce

Tangy peppers

This is a favorite recipe during the summer when bell peppers are abundant. Large batches were prepared in our house when I was a child and enjoyed cold throughout the day, for lunch, dinner or as a snack with bread. I make lots of it when the family comes round for a barbecue, or to have with cold roast meat. Once cooked, the longer you leave these peppers, the better the flavor. They are ideal for summer entertaining. Serve with lots of bread to mop up the juices.

Heat the extra-virgin olive oil in a large frying pan, add all the pepper strips and cook over medium-high heat until the skins are golden-brown. Add the anchovy fillets, if using, the garlic, olives and capers. Stir in the sugar, then add the vinegar and allow to evaporate. Reduce the heat to medium, cover with a lid and cook for about 5 minutes, or until the peppers are tender. Season to taste with salt and pepper and sprinkle over the parsley. Serve hot or cold, garnished with the parsley.

Insalata di pane bagnato

Bread salad

- - - - - - - - - - - - - - - - -

SERVES 4

3 tbsp red wine vinegar

4 slices of good country bread, about
½ inch/1cm thick

1 garlic clove, peeled

4 firm plum tomatoes, sliced

1 red onion, thinly sliced

1 small yellow bell pepper, deseeded and cut
into strips

3oz/85g cucumber, thinly sliced

2 celery stalks with leaves, thinly sliced

a handful of fresh basil leaves

6 tbsp extra-virgin olive oil, plus extra to drizzle

salt and freshly ground black pepper

a pinch of dried oregano

- - - - - - - - - - - - - - - - -

This recipe has peasant origins. During the warmer season in areas of southern and central Italy, farmers would wet pieces of stale bread with homemade vinegar and eat them with whatever produce was available in the fields – tomatoes, cucumber, peppers. This makes a lovely, light meal and is very healthy. The vinegar really enhances the salad and makes you want to eat more. My daughter Olivia loves vinegar and raw crunchy vegetables, so why not try it out on your children for a healthy lunch? I'm sure they'll be impressed with all the wonderful colors of the salad and, of course, you can substitute other vegetables, depending on what you and your family prefer.

Dilute the vinegar with 4 tbsp water. Place a slice of bread on each serving plate. Rub the bread with garlic and drizzle with the vinegar mixture.

Place the sliced tomatoes, onion, pepper, cucumber, celery and basil leaves in a bowl, add the extra-virgin olive oil, season with the salt, pepper and oregano and toss well.

Divide the salad between the slices of bread and leave to rest for about 10 minutes. Drizzle with extra-virgin olive oil and serve.

Zucchini al cartoccio

Zucchini chips with mint and vinegar

SERVES 4

2 tbsp red wine vinegar
1 garlic clove, peeled
500g/1lb 2oz zucchini, cut into
batons 1½ inch/4cm long
a handful of fresh mint leaves
plain (all-purpose) flour, to dust
good vegetable or seed oil, to deep-fry
salt

These Italian-type French fries are a great way to entice young children to eat green vegetables. This is a popular method of cooking zucchini in Italy. I have added mint and a drizzle of vinegar to enhance the flavor of the zucchini. It's a really tasty side dish, makes a great snack, or can even be served at children's parties. Try to serve the chips as soon as they are cooked or they will lose their crispiness.

Put the vinegar and garlic in a bowl, cover and leave to marinate for at least 2 hours.

Dust the zucchini and mint in the flour, then shake off any excess. Heat the vegetable oil in a large saucepan or deep-fryer until a small piece of bread dropped in sizzles immediately. Fry the zucchini and mint until golden and crispy. Drain on kitchen towel. Sprinkle with salt and drizzle with the garlic-infused vinegar, then serve immediately.

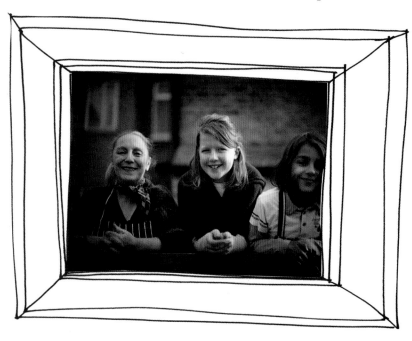

Insalata di pinzimonio

Crunchy salad

SERVES 4

2 fennel bulbs, trimmed and sliced
2 celery hearts, sliced
5$\frac{1}{2}$oz/150g radishes, sliced

for the dressing
4 tbsp extra-virgin olive oil
3 tbsp lemon juice
salt and freshly ground black pepper

Pinzimonio is the Italian equivalent of crudités, a selection of raw vegetables that are dipped in good extra-virgin olive oil, salt and pepper and often served as antipasto or at parties. I remember in Italy the first spring vegetables were so fresh and flavorful that all you needed was some extra-virgin olive oil and a little salt. My father loved fennel and he would often eat raw chunks of it after a meal; he said it refreshed him and aided digestion. Fennel, celery and radishes are commonly included in this healthy, light vegetarian antipasto, which I have made into a crunchy salad with the addition of lemon juice in the dressing. If you prefer, you may omit the lemon juice and add more extra-virgin olive oil. I also like lots of freshly ground black pepper. For maximum flavor, use very fresh vegetables, organic if possible.

Place the fennel, celery and radish in a large bowl. Whisk all the dressing ingredients together until the mixture thickens slightly, then pour over the salad and toss well.

Caponata

Sicilian sweet and sour eggplant

This traditional Sicilian dish is based on eggplant, a popular vegetable on this southern Italian island. A lot of Sicilian dishes have Arab influences, and this accounts for the combination of the sweet and sour ingredients that really enhances the flavor of the eggplants and onions. This dish is often served cold as a starter, or as a side dish to accompany meat and fish. In the Naples area, an equivalent is known as *cianfotta*. I remember at the end of summer, when eggplants were abundant, we would often make a version of this and eat it cold with bread. To enjoy the dish at its best, make it the day before you plan to eat it and leave it in the fridge overnight for all the flavors to settle and infuse the eggplant.

Heat the extra-virgin olive oil in a large frying pan and fry the eggplants over medium-high heat until golden. Remove and drain on kitchen towel.

Reduce the heat to medium, then add the onions to the same pan and sweat until softened. Add the capers and olives and cook for 2 minutes. Stir in the diluted tomato purée and cook for about 5 minutes, until it begins to thicken slightly. Dilute the sugar in the vinegar and add to the pan along with the pine kernels, raisins and eggplant. Reduce the heat to low, half-cover with a lid and cook for 20 minutes. Season with salt and pepper to taste. Serve hot or cold, garnished with the celery leaves. If serving cold, refrigerate and remove 30 minutes before serving.

Carciofi alla Napoletana

Artichokes with olives and capers

SERVES 4

4 globe artichokes

juice of 1 lemon

4 tbsp extra-virgin olive oil

1 garlic clove, roughly chopped

a handful of fresh parsley, roughly chopped

1oz/25g pitted black olives, roughly chopped

1 tbsp capers, roughly chopped

5 tbsp/75ml dry white wine

1¼ cups/300ml hot vegetable stock

freshly ground black pepper

Italians love the versatile globe artichoke, especially in the south, where it grows in abundance. They can be fried, roasted, filled, braised or eaten raw. I remember the artichoke vendors in my home village selling them roasted and the streets being filled with smoke; the smell was intoxicating and immediately made me hungry. This would always entice my father to buy some fresh from the market and cook them in a variety of ways. It was always his job to clean and cook them and my mother was never allowed to interfere. He would often braise them, as in this recipe, with olives and capers.

Clean the artichokes, removing the bottom outer leaves and trimming the tops. Cut off the stems and peel them, then slice lengthways and place in a bowl of water with the lemon juice (this will prevent discoloration). Cut the artichokes into quarters, discarding any hairs, and place them immediately in the lemon water.

Heat the extra-virgin olive oil in a saucepan, add the garlic, parsley, olives and capers and sweat on a medium heat for 1 minute. Drain the artichokes, add to the pan and stir-fry for 3 minutes. Stir in the wine, then add the hot stock and some black pepper. Half-cover with a lid and cook over medium heat for about 20 minutes. Remove the lid and continue to cook for 10 minutes, until the artichokes are cooked through and the liquid has reduced by at least half.

SERVES 4

2lb 4oz/1kg new baby potatoes
salt and freshly ground black pepper
4 tbsp extra-virgin olive oil
1 garlic clove, thinly sliced
2 bay leaves
a pinch of dried oregano
leaves from 1 fresh rosemary sprig
leaves from 1 fresh thyme sprig

Le patate arrosto di Adriana

Adriana's roast potatoes

I love these roast potatoes. My sister Adriana makes them whenever she roasts meat. The herbs really bring out the taste of the new potatoes. They're easy to prepare and quick to cook.

Preheat the oven to 425°F/220°C/gas mark 7.

Wash and scrub the potatoes, but do not peel them. Place in a saucepan of lightly salted water, bring to a boil and cook for 5 minutes. Remove from the heat and drain. Place in a roasting pan together with the rest of the ingredients and, using your hands, toss well. Cover with foil and roast for 10 minutes, then remove the foil and roast for a further 15 minutes, until golden and cooked through.

Insalata di bietole rosse con cipollotti

Beetroot and spring onion salad

SERVES 4–6

1lb 9oz/700g beetroot
a small bunch of spring onions (scallions),
shredded

for the dressing

8 tbsp extra-virgin olive oil
3 tbsp red wine vinegar
2 garlic cloves, thinly sliced
a handful of chives, finely chopped
salt and freshly ground black pepper, to taste

Although more commonly associated with Eastern Europe than Italy, beetroot was a favorite of my mother's. Perhaps it was her Russian ancestry that made her love it. She would often have it simply dressed with some extra-virgin olive oil or, when she had a glut, she would boil it in vinegar and preserve it in lots of olive oil. It is also one of my wife

Liz's favorite vegetables, and she loves it in a simple salad with spring onions (scallions). My daughters, too, have taken a liking to beetroot and we look forward to the end of summer when my friend Paolo brings wonderful organic beetroot in all shapes, sizes and colors from his garden.

Wash and scrub the beetroot under cold running water. Place it in a saucepan with plenty of cold water and bring to a boil, then reduce the heat to low and simmer for about $1\frac{1}{2}$ hours, until the beetroot is tender.

Meanwhile, combine all the dressing ingredients together in a small bowl.

Drain the beetroot and pat dry with a clean cloth. Remove the skins with the help of the cloth. Cut the flesh into quarters or slices, depending on the size of the beetroot, and place in a serving bowl with the spring onions. Pour the dressing over and leave for 20 minutes. Discard the garlic slices before serving if you wish.

PANE

DOUGH

There is an old Italian saying, 'Buono come il pane' (literally 'as good as bread'), when talking about a good person because that is exactly what bread is. For me, bread is everything. When you have it, you need little else. It is healthy, nutritious and feeds the soul. In Italy it is served at each meal and bought fresh each day from the panetteria (bakery).

The smell of freshly baked bread evokes warm feelings of home and family. My mother used to make it every Thursday. It was a ritual; she would light the wood-fired oven the night before and wake up extra early the next morning to stoke the fire. As the loaves baked, the smell would slowly waft through the house and immediately had me out of bed and into the kitchen. A few cooked loaves would be on the kitchen table, others still in the oven. She would often add sugar and perhaps some dried fruit and citrus zest to the remaining dough to make a pane dolce (sweet bread, see page 195). I loved to tear the first loaf apart and eat the warm bread — the taste was heavenly.

Long after we had all left the family home, my mother would make bread when we went to visit. In those early days, when I travelled to and from Italy by train, she would often enrich it with ham, salami and cheese, and give it to me for the journey back. Being a young man, I didn't really want to have a knapsack, but she always insisted and I was so glad, because on that long, melancholic journey through France during the night, when I felt lonely and hungry, the taste of my mother's bread and the memories of home it evoked soon filled me with warmth and happiness.

Bread means tradition. It is made all over the world, in different ways, but the basic ingredients are the same. In Italy it is never thrown away — that would be a sin, and old wives' tales said that if you did, bad luck would be bestowed upon you. Bread was thought to be holy food and a gift from God. Leftover, stale bread was always used up, for breadcrumbs, in panzanella (bread salad), as fillings, or put back in the oven to double-bake as a hard biscuit-type bread.

I love to bake bread. In fact, I should have been a baker. A few years ago I had a wood-fired oven built in my garden and have tried to recreate the look and atmosphere of the one we had at home when I was a child. When I get lost in nostalgia for my childhood, this little corner of the garden fills me with warm feelings. When I plan to bake, I get up very early in the morning to light the oven, and I love to hear the crackling of the fire almost speaking to me. I prepare the flour, yeast, salt and water and always make sure I talk to the dough before leaving it to rise. If I talk nicely to it, it will rise well and produce excellent bread!

In Italy we make a variety of savory breads, such as the pane pasquale, a round loaf filled with cheese and salami and topped with boiled eggs to represent Easter. When I was a child, savory breads were common in rural areas as a quick and easy lunch for farmers whilst working in the fields. These are still made today to be enjoyed on picnics and journeys, just like my mother used to do for me. And the famous Italian Christmas cake, panettone, is made from dough.

I like to make pizza when friends come round. I usually make tons of dough – Liz always tells me off for making too much, but I just can't help it. I get everyone involved and ask all my guests to top their own pizza and bake it in the very hot oven. I love to see their amazed expressions when, after a few minutes, a delicious hot pizza emerges. It's great being outside because you can make a real mess and it doesn't matter. I shape any remaining dough into loaves and bake these towards the end of the day, so all my guests can take some home. There are usually lots more left, so I send the girls off with loaves for the neighbors (but of course, not before they have had a slice of freshly baked warm bread smeared with lots of butter). The next day for breakfast, they always ask for 'Toast with Daddy's bread!' I love to see them just as excited as I was when my mother used to bake bread.

MAKES 1 LOAF/SERVES 4–6

¹/₄oz/12g fresh yeast

scant 1¹/₂ cups/325ml
lukewarm water

3¹/₂ cups/500g Italian '00' flour
or strong plain (all-purpose bread) flour,
plus extra to dust

2 tsp salt

Imposto per pane

Bread dough

So simple and yet so nutritious and wholesome. There is nothing more satisfying to me than making my own bread. This recipe is for a plain loaf, or it can be formed into rolls. It is one of the nicest things you can make for your family. It will keep for about a week, or even longer, and is great sliced and made into bruschetta or toasted for breakfast.

Dissolve the yeast in the water. Combine the flour and salt on a clean work surface or in a large bowl, make a well in the center, then gradually pour in the dissolved yeast liquid and mix to form a soft but not sticky dough – if necessary, add a little more lukewarm water. Lightly flour a clean work surface and knead the dough well for about 5 minutes, until smooth and elastic. Place on a clean tea towel,

brush the top with water to prevent it from drying out, then cover with another clean, slightly damp tea towel. Leave to rise in a warm place for about 30 minutes, or until the dough has doubled in size.

Shape the dough into a loaf and put in a 1lb/450g loaf pan, or on a flat baking sheet. Cover and leave to rise in a warm place for 30 minutes. Preheat the oven to 480°F/250°C/gas mark 9.

Place the loaf in the oven, reduce the temperature to 475°F/240°C/gas mark 8 and bake for about 20 minutes, until golden. To test if the loaf is ready, remove from the loaf pan (if using) and gently tap it on the bottom – if it sounds hollow, it is ready. Leave to cool on a wire rack. It is very tempting to slice it as soon as you can handle it and spread it with butter!

MAKES 2 LARGE PIZZAS

1 quantity of pizza dough (see page 183)
dried breadcrumbs, flour or semolina, to dust

for the topping

3 tbsp extra-virgin olive oil, plus extra, to drizzle
1 garlic clove, finely chopped
1/2 red chilli (optional), roughly chopped
9oz/250g tender-stem broccoli, stems trimmed
9oz/250g pork sausages, roughly chopped
(skinless, if preferred)
salt and freshly ground black pepper, to taste
14oz/400g can chopped plum tomatoes

La pizza di Olivia

Olivia's pizza

Olivia's favorite food is pizza, but she really enjoys sausages and broccoli too, so we combined them together. (Sausages with broccoli is actually a very common dish in southern Italy; the broccoli used is the *cime di rapa* (rape tops), slightly bitter-tasting with lots of leaves, which are also cooked.) This pizza is highly nutritious and filling, and really a meal on its own.

Make the pizza dough as described on page 183.

Preheat the oven to its highest setting.

Heat the extra-virgin olive oil in a large frying pan, add the garlic and chilli, if using, and sweat over medium–high heat for a couple of minutes. Add the broccoli, sausage and salt to taste and sauté for 1 minute. Cover with a lid, reduce the heat to medium and cook for 15 minutes.

Meanwhile, prepare the bases. Sprinkle a little flour on a clean work surface and, using your fingers, spread a piece of dough into a circle roughly 11–12 inches/28–30cm in diameter. The dough must be very thin, but be careful not to tear it. Repeat with the other ball of dough. Sprinkle some breadcrumbs, flour or semolina over 2 large flat baking sheets and place the pizza bases on them.

Remove the sausage and broccoli from the heat. Put the tomatoes in a bowl, season with salt and pepper and a drizzle of extra-virgin olive oil, and stir. Spoon the tomatoes over the pizza bases, then scatter with the sausages and broccoli and drizzle with extra-virgin olive oil. Reduce the oven to 425°F/220°C/gas mark 7 and bake the pizzas for about 8 minutes, or until cooked.

La pizza di Chloe

Chloe's pizza

MAKES 2 LARGE PIZZAS

¹/₄oz/10g fresh yeast or 1 x 7g sachet of dried

scant 1¹/₂ cups/325ml lukewarm water

3¹/₂ cups/500g strong plain (all-purpose bread) flour, plus extra to dust

2 tsp salt

dried breadcrumbs, flour or semolina, to dust

14oz/400g can chopped plum tomatoes, optional

for the topping

extra-virgin olive oil, to drizzle

2 balls of mozzarella, roughly chopped

6 slices of Parma ham, roughly torn

2 handfuls of rocket

The topping on this pizza includes Chloe's favorite ingredients. This type of *pizza bianca* is not traditional, but has become popular in *pizzerie* all over Italy during the last 20 years.

Dissolve the fresh yeast in the water (if you are using easy-blend/active dry yeast, just mix it in with the flour). Combine the flour and salt for the dough in a large bowl, then gradually add the dissolved yeast liquid (or dried yeast and water), mixing well to form a dough. Shape the dough into a ball, cover with a cloth and leave to rest for 5 minutes.

Knead the dough for 10 minutes, until smooth and elastic, then split in half. Knead each piece for 2 minutes, then shape into a ball. Sprinkle some flour on a clean tea towel or baking sheet and place the dough on it. Cover with a slightly damp cloth and leave to rise in a warm place for at least 1 hour.

Preheat the oven to its highest setting.

Sprinkle a little flour on a clean work surface and, using your fingers, spread a piece of dough into a circle roughly 11–12 inches/28–30cm in diameter. The dough must be very thin, but be careful not to tear it. Repeat with the other ball of dough. Sprinkle some breadcrumbs, flour or semolina over 2 large flat baking sheets and place the pizza bases on them.

If using the tomatoes, put them in a bowl, season with salt and pepper and a drizzle of extra-virgin olive oil, and stir. Spoon the tomatoes over the pizza bases (if not using tomatoes, just drizzle the bases with extra-virgin olive oil). Arrange the mozzarella pieces on top, followed by the Parma ham. Reduce the oven temperature to 425°F/220°C/gas mark 7 and bake the pizzas for about 8 minutes, or until cooked. Remove from the oven, top with the rocket and drizzle with some more extra-virgin olive oil.

1 quantity of basic bread dough (see page 177)

6 tbsp extra-virgin olive oil, plus extra to grease

1 large red onion, thinly sliced

1lb 2oz/500g canned cherry tomatoes

salt and freshly ground black pepper

1oz/25g anchovies in oil, drained

2¹⁄₄oz/60g caciocavallo cheese, roughly chopped

Sfincione Siciliano

Sicilian focaccia

The *sfincione* is a traditional focaccia from Palermo in Sicily, and was originally baked by the nuns at the San Vito monastery and served at Christmas as a richer variety of bread. In modern Palermo it is found in *rosticcerie*, and sold by street vendors from their three-wheeler vehicles. The word '*sfincione*' derives from '*sfincia*', meaning 'something very soft', which indeed the dough is. Normally, sardines are added to the rich tomato topping, but I have substituted anchovies instead. Caciocavallo cheese is a typical southern Italian cheese that can be found in good delis; however, you can use provolone or Parmesan instead. This is a delicious snack, perfect for the whole family to share.

Make the bread dough as described on page 177.

While the bread is rising, make the sauce. Heat 2 tbsp extra-virgin olive oil in a saucepan, add the onion and sweat over medium heat until softened. Add the tomatoes and season with salt and pepper, then cover with a lid, reduce the heat to low and cook for 20 minutes. Five minutes before the end of cooking time add the anchovies. Preheat the oven to 425°F/220°C/gas mark 7.

When the bread dough has risen, add the remaining extra-virgin olive oil to it and, using your hands, knead it in well. Initially you may feel that the oil is not being absorbed, but continue to knead for about 10 minutes and it will be evenly distributed.

Gently grease a 11 inch/28cm round baking sheet with olive oil and place the dough on it. Using your fingers, spread it around to the edges. Scatter the cheese all over the dough and top with the tomato and anchovy sauce.

Reduce the oven temperature to 400°F/200°C/gas mark 6 and bake the sfincione for 35 minutes. Transfer to a wire rack and leave to cool.

Ciambella all'acciughe e olive

Anchovy and olive bread

- - - - - - - - - - - - - - - - - -

SERVES 4

4 tbsp extra-virgin olive oil, plus extra to grease

3oz/85g anchovies in oil, drained

4 tbsp/50g butter

3^{1}/$_{2}$ cups/500g '00' flour or strong plain (all-purpose bread) flour, plus extra to dust

1 x 7g sachet of dried yeast

4 eggs

3oz/85g mixed green and black olives, pitted and finely chopped

- - - - - - - - - - - - - - - - - -

Ciambella usually means a sweet ring cake, but nowadays it refers to savory cakes too. This recipe uses bread dough enriched with eggs, with the addition of olives and anchovies. It can be eaten on its own, with cured meats and cheese, or as an accompaniment to main meals.

Heat 2 tbsp extra-virgin olive oil in a small frying pan. Add the anchovies (keeping 2 aside for later) and cook over low heat until they dissolve. Remove from the heat and stir in the butter until melted.

Combine the flour, yeast and eggs in a large bowl. Add the anchovy mixture and olives and mix well to form a smooth dough. Knead on a lightly floured surface for 10 minutes, then cover with a clean tea towel and leave in a warm place for 1^{1}/$_{2}$ hours.

Preheat the oven to 425°F/220°C/gas mark 7. Grease a 20cm/8-inch ring cake pan with extra-virgin olive oil and line with greaseproof paper, then grease the paper with oil.

Knead the dough for a minute, then shape it to fit the tin. Finely slice lengthways the remaining 2 anchovy fillets. Using a sharp knife, make incisions on top of the bread and insert a sliver of anchovy into each cut. Bake for 40 minutes, then leave to rest for 5 minutes. Slice and serve.

Calzoncini

Small calzoni filled with cheese

- - - - - - - - - - - - - - - - - - - -

MAKES 10 CALZONCINI

1 x 7g sachet of dried yeast

5 tbsp/75ml lukewarm water

1²/₃ cups/250g '00' flour or strong plain
(all-purpose bread) flour, plus extra to dust

1 egg

2 tsp extra-virgin olive oil

good vegetable or seed oil to deep-fry

for the filling

1 tbsp extra-virgin olive oil

a knob of butter

1 red onion, thinly sliced

3¹/₂oz/100g ricotta

3¹/₂oz/100g mozzarella, cut into small cubes

³/₄oz/20g Parmesan, grated

a handful of fresh basil leaves, finely chopped

salt and freshly ground black pepper

- - - - - - - - - - - - - - - - - - -

Calzoncini are a type of filled pizza that are deep-fried. Popular throughout southern Italy, they were a treat my father would buy from the local *rosticcieria* when I was out with him. They were also made at home with leftover bread dough and especially liked by children, who would wait by the stove as the *calzoncini* were lifted out of the oil. They make a lovely nutritious snack and are ideal for children's parties. I have used a traditional filling of red onion and three cheeses, but you could use tomato or ham.

First, make the dough. Dissolve the yeast in the water. Place the flour in a large bowl or on a clean work surface. Make a well in the center and gradually add the yeasted water, egg and extra-virgin olive oil, mixing well to form a smooth dough.

Knead on a lightly floured surface for 10 minutes. Take pieces of dough, each weighing about 1¹/₂oz/40g, and form into balls, then flatten slightly and place on a tray. Cover with a clean tea towel and leave to rise in a warm place for 1 hour.

For the filling, heat the extra-virgin olive oil and butter in a small frying pan, add the onion, cover the pan with a lid and cook on a low heat for about 10 minutes, or until the onion has softened. Remove from the heat and leave to cool.

Combine the ricotta, mozzarella, Parmesan, basil, salt, pepper and cooled onion in a bowl and set aside.

Take each piece of dough and roll out on a lightly floured surface into a circle about 4 inches/10cm in diameter and about ¹/₈ inch/3mm thick. Place a spoonful of filling in the center of each, brush water around the edges and fold the dough over, sealing well – make sure the filling does not escape.

Heat vegetable oil for deep frying in a pan or deep-fryer. When hot, fry the *calzoncini* in batches until golden. Drain on kitchen towel and serve hot or cold.

Sformato di pane alle verdure

Italian vegetable pie

- -

SERVES 6–8

1 x 7g sachet of dried yeast

$^2/_3$ cup/150ml lukewarm water

1$^2/_3$ cups/250g '00' flour or strong plain
(all-purpose bread) flour, plus extra to dust

2 tbsp/25g softened butter, cut
into pieces

for the filling

3 tbsp extra-virgin olive oil, plus extra to brush
and drizzle

1lb 2oz/500g potatoes

salt and freshly ground black pepper

1 small onion, thinly sliced

10$^1/_2$oz/300g zucchini, thinly sliced

4 artichokes preserved in oil, sliced
(reserve 2 tbsp of the oil)

1lb 5oz/600g spinach

2 eggs

1$^3/_4$oz/50g Parmesan, grated

- -

Pies are not normally associated with Italian cooking, but in Campania it is traditional to make a savory pie during Christmas. It is made with leftover bread dough enriched with lard and escarole, mixed with anchovies, capers, pine kernels and olives. The pie is a nutritious snack, which farmers used to take with them to the fields for lunch, and I remember finding a slice in my school lunchbox – a treat my nonna (grandmother) would put in, as she made the pie for my nonno (grandfather), who loved it. I have made a lighter version – and believe me, once you start on a slice, you will want more.

Dissolve the yeast in the water. Combine the flour, butter and a pinch of salt in a large bowl. Make a well in the center, gradually pour in the yeasted water and mix well to form a soft but not sticky dough. Knead on a lightly floured surface for 10 minutes, then form into a ball, cover with a clean tea towel and leave to rise in a warm place for 2 hours.

Preheat the oven to 400°F/200°C/gas mark 6. Lightly grease a baking sheet with olive oil.

Peel the potatoes and slice into rounds about $^1/_4$ inch/5mm thick. Place on the baking sheet, sprinkle with salt and pepper and drizzle with extra-virgin olive oil. Roast for about 15 minutes, until cooked through but firm.

Meanwhile, heat 3 tbsp extra-virgin olive oil in a frying pan, add the onion, then sweat over a medium heat until it has softened. Add the zucchini and sauté over medium heat for 10 minutes until softened. Add the artichokes with their oil and cook for 5 minutes. Add the spinach and salt and pepper to taste, cover with a lid and cook for 5 minutes. Allow to cool.

Increase the oven temperature to 425°F/220°C/gas mark 7. Beat the eggs in a bowl, then stir in the Parmesan and some salt and pepper. Add the cooled vegetables and gently combine.

Line a round 9 inch/23cm diameter pie dish with greaseproof paper. Divide the dough in half. Roll out one half on a lightly floured surface and line the bottom and sides of the pie dish. Arrange the cooked potatoes on the bottom, followed by the vegetable filling. Roll out the other piece of dough and cover the pie, sealing well so that the filling does not escape. Prick all over with a fork and brush with extra-virgin olive oil. Bake in the oven for 30–35 minutes, until golden. Can be eaten hot or cold.

Panini al Parmigiano

Parmesan bread rolls

- -

MAKES 16 ROLLS

3½ cups/500g '0' flour or strong plain (all-purpose bread) flour, plus extra to dust

3oz/85g Parmesan, grated

1 x 7g sachet of dried yeast

2 tsp salt

scant 3 tbsp/40ml extra-virgin olive oil

generous 1 cup/250ml lukewarm water

- -

This recipe came about by mistake – I was once making some bread rolls and instead of salt I grabbed Parmesan. Although annoyed with myself at first, I decided to add more cheese and see what the result would be. Well, they were a success, as you can see by the inclusion of this recipe in the book. The Parmesan gives a really nice taste, as well as making them more nutritious. They're fun to make with the children, who, of course, can make any shape they like.

Put all the dry ingredients into a large bowl or on a clean work surface. Make a well in the center and add the extra-virgin olive oil, then gradually add the water and mix to a smooth dough. Knead for 10 minutes, then cover with a clean tea towel and leave to rise for 1½ hours.

Knead the dough for 1 minute, then divide into small pieces, each weighing about 1½oz/40g. Roll out each piece on a lightly floured surface into a thin sausage about 8½ inch/22cm in length and wrap round into a coil. Using kitchen scissors, snip around the edge for a decorative effect, if desired. Cover and leave to rise for a further 40 minutes.

Preheat the oven to 425°F/220°C/gas mark 7. Lightly flour a non-stick baking sheet.

Place the rolls on the baking sheet and bake for 15–20 minutes, until golden. Cool on a wire rack.

Pane dolce

Sweet bread cake

- - - - - - - - - - - - - - - - - - - -

MAKES 1 X 8-INCH/20CM ROUND CAKE

2 egg yolks

$\frac{1}{3}$ cup/70g caster (superfine) sugar

scant 4 tbsp/50g softened butter, cut into pieces, plus extra to grease

$1\frac{1}{2}$oz/40g mixed candied peel

finely grated zest of 1 orange

a pinch of ground cinnamon

a pinch of salt

$\frac{2}{3}$ cup/about 100g '00' flour or strong plain (all-purpose bread) flour, plus extra to dust

icing sugar, to dust

for the dough

1 x 7g sachet of dried yeast

$\frac{1}{3}$ cup/100ml lukewarm water

$1\frac{2}{3}$ cups/250g '00' flour or strong plain (all-purpose bread) flour

- - - - - - - - - - - - - - - - - - -

Making sweet bread-type cakes is very popular in Italy. It originated as *cucina povera* when people wanted something sweet but could not afford it. My mother and grandmother normally made it with leftover bread dough and added a little sugar, eggs and whatever else was available – dried fruit, lemon or orange zest. It is made all over Italy and known by different names, such as *stiacciata* in Tuscany, or even *focaccia*, as we often called it. The sweetened bread dough was baked and eaten at teatime or at breakfast, dipped into warm milk. It is delicious served toasted with jam and makes an ideal snack for hungry children after school.

For the dough, dissolve the yeast in the water. Place the flour in a large bowl or on a clean work surface. Make a well in the center and gradually add the yeasted water, mixing well to form a smooth dough. Knead on a lightly floured work surface for 10 minutes. Form into a ball, cover with a clean tea towel and leave to rest in a warm place for 1 hour.

Meanwhile, whisk the egg yolks, sugar and butter until creamy. Stir in the candied peel, orange zest, cinnamon and salt. Place the risen dough on a work surface, then flatten with your hands and gradually work the egg mixture into the dough, adding a little flour as you do. You will find this is a sticky operation, but just keep adding the flour gradually and it will become a soft dough.

Lightly grease and flour a 8-inch/20cm round cake tin. Place the dough in the tin, cover with a clean tea towel and leave to rise in a warm place for 1 hour.

Preheat the oven to 375°F/190°C/gas mark 5.

When the dough has risen, bake for 30 minutes, or until golden. Leave to cool in the tin.

To serve, turn out of the tin, dust with icing sugar and slice crossways, as you would bread.

Dolci

SWEETS

When I was a child, dessert was usually fresh fruit. As soon as the main course was over, my mother would put the fruit bowl on the table so we could help ourselves. I loved picking cherries, peaches, apricots, wild strawberries and, my favorite at the end of summer, figs. I always knew where the best fruit was and which tree had the ripest — I checked daily. When I brought home lots of fruit, my mother would transform it into jams, cakes and crostate (tarts), which I would enjoy for merenda (afternoon snack). If I picked morello cherries she would put them in jars with sugar and leave them in the sun for a few days, until the sugar had dissolved and a wonderful cherry syrup was left, which would be used in ice cream and pasticiotto (a type of cherry pie).

Most desserts, cakes and biscuits were made at home by women. My grandmother's speciality was apple cake, my mother's was fruit tart and my sisters would experiment with biscuits, fruit salads and ice cream. Sweet treats were usually made from leftovers — bread dough was used to make pan dolce or sweet pies and a glut of fruit would go into tarts and cakes. We also enjoyed ricotta as a dessert; this was freshly made and sometimes served warm with a little sugar or cinnamon sprinkled over the top. A lot of southern Italian cakes and pastries include ricotta — for instance the Sicilian cassata (see page 214) and cannoli (little filled tubes of pastry dough), as well as tarts and cakes.

There was a small pasticcieria in our village of Minori, and sometimes, usually for a special occasion, we would buy cakes there. We knew the family who owned it and now and then I helped with odd jobs such as skinning almonds (not the most glamorous of tasks); it was interesting to watch the pasticciere (pastry chef) at work. The pasticcieria has grown considerably since I left and is now quite a famous spot to enjoy their lemon cakes. I love desserts and have a very sweet tooth; I don't have much time to make them these days, but when I do I tend to recreate my mother's fruit crostate (see page 210).

Gelatina di vino bianco con frutti di bosco

White wine jelly with fruits of the forest and strawberry sauce

SERVES 4

1 leaf or sheet of gelatin
scant 1 cup/200ml dry white wine
$^1/_3$ cup/70g caster (superfine) sugar
$^1/_2$ clove
$^1/_2$ inch/1cm piece of cinnamon stick
1oz/25g raspberries
1oz/25g blueberries
4 fresh mint leaves, plus extra to decorate
4 tsp good natural yogurt

for the strawberry sauce

3$^1/_2$oz/100g strawberries, hulled,
plus extra, sliced, to decorate
juice of $^1/_2$ lemon
2 tbsp caster (superfine) sugar

Jelly (jello) in desserts is not traditionally Italian, but it has become popular in restaurants and at home, particularly for children's parties. I like this recipe for summer entertaining, to make use of the season's berries. It looks stunning served in small liqueur glasses. Because of the alcohol content, the portions are small. For children, substitute freshly squeezed orange or elderflower juice for the wine.

Place the gelatin in a bowl of cold water to soften. Meanwhile, combine the wine, sugar, clove and cinnamon stick in a small saucepan and place over a medium heat. Bring to a boil, then boil rapidly for 3 minutes, until the sugar has dissolved. Remove from the heat and remove and discard the clove and cinnamon. Drain the gelatin, squeeze out the excess water, then stir the gelatin into the liquid and leave to cool.

Meanwhile, blend all the ingredients for the sauce to a smooth consistency in a food processor, then cover and refrigerate.

Divide the cooled jelly liquid between 4 x 3$^1/_2$fl oz/100ml liqueur glasses, filling them to just over halfway. Drop a few raspberries, blueberries and a mint leaf in each glass. Place in the fridge for 6 hours, or until the jelly has set. When set, top the jellies with the strawberry sauce, then a dollop of yogurt, and decorate with strawberry slices and mint leaves. Cover and store in the fridge until required.

SERVES 4–6

2 peaches, pitted

2 white peaches, pitted

4 apricots, pitted

4 kiwi fruit, peeled

7oz/200g strawberries, hulled

3½oz/100g blueberries

½ cup/100g caster
(superfine) sugar

juice of ½ lemon

juice of 1 large orange

a few fresh mint leaves, to decorate

Macedonia estiva

Summer fruit salad

For me, fruit is the best dessert, and what better way to celebrate summer than by putting all the season's fruits together. *Macedonia* (fruit salad) has always been popular in Italy. Different fruits are used depending on the season, but sugar and citrus fruits are typically used for the dressing. Once the fruit has been left to macerate, a lovely sweet syrup develops and enhances the taste of the fruit. This simple summer dessert is delicious served with lemon sorbet (sherbet), if desired, and can be enjoyed by the whole family or when entertaining. Easy, nutritious and packed with vitamins, it makes a refreshing end to a meal.

Slice the peaches, white peaches, apricots, kiwi fruit and strawberries and place in a large bowl with the blueberries.

Combine the sugar with the lemon and orange juices in a small bowl and mix well until the sugar has dissolved. Pour over the fruit, decorate with mint leaves, cover and allow to macerate for at least 30 minutes before serving.

Il gelato della nonna Fausta

Nonna Fausta's ice cream

- - - - - - - - - - - - - - - -

SERVES 4

2 egg yolks
1¼ cups/250g caster (superfine) sugar
generous 2 cups/500ml milk
2½ inch/6cm vanilla pod (bean), split
6 slices of unwaxed lemon peel
biscuits such as savoiardi, to serve

- - - - - - - - - - - - - - - -

This recipe comes from my wife Liz's grandmother, who used to make it for her during the annual summer visit to Italy. Two aluminum trays of it were always in the freezer: one vanilla and one chocolate. This is the traditional way of making ice cream and, according to Nonna Fausta, the secret is getting the sugar content right. When I recreated this recipe, it took me back to my childhood days and my immediate reaction was 'sapore genuino' ('it has the genuine taste!').

Beat together the egg yolks and sugar until creamy. Add the milk and whisk well. Add the vanilla pod and lemon peel. Pour into a saucepan, place over a gentle heat, stirring well all the time, until almost boiling. Remove from the heat and leave to cool, then remove the vanilla pod and lemon peel.

Place in a plastic container and freeze for 6 hours, removing from the freezer every 20 minutes to stir gently but thoroughly. Continue to do this for about 6 hours. (Alternatively, once your cream has cooled, place in the ice-cream maker and follow the instructions, then put in the freezer.)

Serve the ice cream in scoops in glasses with savoiardi biscuits.

For chocolate ice cream

To make a chocolate ice cream, make as above, but omit the vanilla and lemon peel. When you remove the pan from the heat, gradually add 1oz/25g good sifted unsweetened cocoa powder, whisking well to avoid lumps. Then proceed with the freezing process by hand or machine.

MAKES ABOUT 10 POPSICLES

5½oz/150g strawberries, hulled

3 egg yolks

⅓ cup/75g caster
(superfine) sugar

a pinch of salt

⅔ cup/150ml milk

⅓ cup/100ml heavy cream

6 fresh mint leaves

finely grated zest of 1 large
unwaxed lemon

Ghiaccioli al limone e fragole

Lemon and strawberry popsicles

The consistency of these popsicles is more like ice cream, while the combination of lemon, strawberries and a slight mint infusion works really well. Placing thin slices of strawberry on the sides of the molds gives a pretty effect when the popsicles are unmolded. Make sure you get good molds, as it can be tricky to remove the popsicles when set.

(If you prefer, you can make the mixture in a container and serve as ice cream instead.) The children will enjoy making these with you.

Slice half the strawberries very finely and arrange on the sides of 10 x 2.7oz/80ml ice pop molds. Immediately freeze for 30 minutes. Finely chop the remaining strawberries and set aside.

Using an electric whisk, whisk the egg yolks, sugar and salt together in a bowl until creamy and the sugar has dissolved.

Place the milk, cream and mint leaves in a saucepan and gently heat (do not boil). Remove from the heat and leave to cool slightly, then stir in the egg mixture. Return to a low heat and cook for about 1 minute, stirring all the time, until slightly thickened. Remove from the heat and stir in the chopped strawberries and lemon zest. Pour into the molds and freeze for at least 6 hours.

Semifreddo di zabaglione con salsa di fragole

Zabaglione semifreddo with strawberry sauce

4 egg yolks

generous ¼ cup/60g caster (superfine) sugar

⅔ cup/150ml Marsala

scant 1 cup/200ml heavy cream

for the strawberry sauce

5½oz/150g strawberries, hulled

2 tbsp/25g caster (superfine) sugar

1 tbsp lemon juice

A type of zabaglione was made for me most mornings when I was in a hurry and would not sit down to breakfast. My mother would whisk up an egg, some sugar and a little hot milk in a cup. Often, if I left the house without it, she would come after me with cup in hand and I would have to drink it all up, sometimes in front of my friends, which embarrassed me. However, as a treat, I remember her telling me she would add a drop of Marsala. She insisted this was a quick but highly nutritious breakfast, which would give me lots of energy. With these few simple ingredients, I came up with a delicious semifreddo. It can be made in one container or, if you want to impress guests for a dinner party, individual ones made in paper cups or dariole molds look lovely too.

For the sauce, blend all the ingredients to a smooth consistency in a food processor, then cover and place in the fridge.

For the zabaglione, whisk together the egg yolks and sugar in a heatproof bowl, then place over a saucepan of gently simmering water and whisk for 5 minutes. Gradually add the Marsala, whisking well, until the mixture has doubled in size. Remove from the heat and leave to cool. Whisk the heavy cream until stiff, then fold into the egg mixture.

Line a rectangular plastic or silicone 6 x 4-inch/15 x 10cm mold with plastic wrap and pour in the zabaglione. Freeze for 3 hours.

When required, remove from the freezer and leave to stand for a minute, then tip out on a plate, divide into 4 portions and serve with the strawberry sauce.

Meringhe al caffè

Coffee meringues

My wife Liz's grandmother often made meringues for the grandchildren at teatime. To give the meringues a twist, I have added coffee, and these go really well with a cup of freshly made steaming espresso, ideally served after a meal. If you don't like coffee, especially if making this for children, substitute water for the espresso (although my daughter Olivia loves these). You can make more by increasing the quantities; the meringues can be stored in an airtight container for about a month. They are great for people with celiac disease.

Preheat the oven to 250°F/120°C/gas mark ¹/₂.

Line a baking sheet with non-stick greaseproof paper. Whisk the egg whites in a clean glass bowl until stiff peaks form.

Put the sugar and espresso coffee in a small saucepan and cook on a low heat, stirring all the time, until it boils, then boil and stir for 2 minutes. Remove from the heat and gradually add to the stiffened egg whites, whisking until it is well combined.

Place spoonfuls of the meringue on the prepared baking sheet and bake for 2 hours, or until the meringues have dried out and look smooth and shiny. Cool on a wire rack, then store in an airtight container.

1¹⁄₄ cups/175g plain (all-purpose) flour, plus extra to dust

6 tbsp/75g cold butter, plus extra to grease

¹⁄₃ cup/75g caster (superfine) sugar

finely grated zest of 1 unwaxed lemon

2 egg yolks

1 x generous 1 cup/250ml of strawberry jam (see page 232)

1 egg, beaten

icing (confectioner's) sugar, sifted, to dust

Crostata di Mamma

My mom's jam tart

Simple homemade jam or fruit tarts like this one are common all over Italy, made by mammas for their children, usually for *merenda* (teatime). My mom used to make this tart for us, filled with her delicious strawberry jam. The pastry is simple to make and, if you make a large quantity, it can be frozen to use later. By preparing your own pastry and filling, you can create a simple and nutritious sweet treat.

To make the pastry, put the flour on a clean work surface and rub in the butter until the mixture resembles breadcrumbs. Add the sugar, lemon zest and egg yolks and mix well to form a smooth dough. Shape into a ball, wrap in plastic wrap and leave in the fridge for 30 minutes, or until required.

Preheat the oven to 350°F/180°C/gas mark 4. Grease a round 8 inch/20cm tart pan with a little butter.

Roll out the pastry on a lightly floured surface and use to line the greased tart pan. Cut off the trimmings and form them into a ball, then roll out and cut into 12 strips.

Fill the pastry case with the jam, then arrange the strips over the tart in a lattice pattern. Brush the strips with the beaten egg, then bake the tart for 25 minutes, until lightly golden.

Leave to cool slightly, then sprinkle with icing sugar and serve.

Biscotti di polenta agli agrumi

Citrus polenta biscuits

Using polenta (cornmeal) in desserts has become fashionable, and it is often made into cakes and biscuits. Apart from being delicious, with that extra crunch that polenta flour gives, these biscuits are a perfect sweet treat for anyone suffering from wheat intolerance. Simple to make and quick to bake, they are an ideal accompaniment to ice cream (see Il gelato della nonna Fausta, page 204) or to enjoy with a cup of tea. Space them well apart on the baking tray, as they spread during cooking; if necessary, bake in batches.

Preheat the oven to 350°F/180°C/gas mark 4. Combine the polenta, cornflour, sugar and orange and lemon zests in a bowl. Make a well in the center, pour in the melted butter and beaten eggs and stir well. Cover and refrigerate for 20 minutes, until it becomes a little firmer.

Line 2 large baking trays with non-stick greaseproof paper. Place ¹/₂ tbsp dollops on the paper, spacing them at least 2¹/₂ inches/6cm apart. Bake for 12 minutes, until the edges turn golden. Leave to cool slightly before serving.

Torta di mela di Nonna Genoveffa

Granny Genoveffa's apple cake

- -

SERVES 4–6

6 tbsp/85g unsalted softened butter, plus extra
to grease

3 Granny Smith apples

juice and finely grated zest of 1 small
unwaxed lemon

3 eggs

³/₄ cup/150g caster (superfine) sugar

1 vanilla pod

generous 2 cups/300g self-raising
(self-rising) flour

- -

This is a homely cake that, while baking, fills the house with a wonderful aroma. In the fall I would bring home basketfuls of apples and always made sure I gave lots to my grandma because I knew she would make this cake. She would bake several to give to family and friends. I gave the recipe to my wife Liz, who now makes it, and I can't tell you how quickly the slices disappear, often still warm. I have used Granny Smith apples, but any will suffice and if you prefer you can substitute pears, plums or apricots – a cake for every season.

Preheat the oven to 350°F/180°C/gas mark 4. Grease a round, 8 inch/20cm diameter, loose-bottomed cake pan with a little butter, then line with non-stick greaseproof paper.

Peel and core the apples, chop them into medium chunks and put them in a bowl. Squeeze over the lemon juice to avoid discoloration and set aside.

Whisk together the eggs and sugar in a large bowl until light and fluffy. Add the butter and whisk until well combined. Split the vanilla pod with a sharp knife and scoop out the seeds with the tip of the knife, then add them to the bowl. Sift in the flour, then fold it in. Add and fold in the apples and lemon zest.

Pour the mixture into the prepared pan and bake for about 40 minutes, or until golden and springy to the touch. Remove from the oven and allow to cool in the tin. To serve, unmold from the tin and place on a serving plate. Slice and enjoy with tea or coffee.

Cassattine

Mini cassata cakes

MAKES 12 SMALL CASSATE

icing (confectioner's) sugar, sifted, to dust

12oz/350g marzipan

scant 3 tbsp/40ml Marsala

sugared flowers, silver balls, angelica and candied peel, to decorate

for the sponge

2 eggs

1/3 cup/100g caster (superfine) sugar

scant 1/2 cup/75g plain (all-purpose) flour, sifted

1 tsp baking powder, sifted

for the filling

1/3 cup/100ml double heavy cream

7oz/200g ricotta

1/4 cup/60g generous caster (superfine) sugar

3oz/85g candied peel

1 1/2oz/40g plain (semisweet) chocolate drops or finely chopped chocolate

---

This recipe is a labor of love. These cakes take time and patience to prepare, but believe me they're worth it. They are traditionally Sicilian, and were first introduced to our family by my aunt Maria. Her husband would often go on business to Sicily and return with tales of this wonderful dessert, and he once bought her kilos of Sicilian almonds. With what she was told and the almonds she had, she decided to give these a go – and what better occasion than my sister Filomena's wedding? Instead of making a large cake, she made hundreds of little ones, and beautifully decorated them all with flowers made of candied fruit; it took her at least 2 days. They were a joy to look at and tasted delicious. When you have made them, leave them overnight in the fridge – they are even more delectable when left to settle for a while.

For the sponge, follow the method for the Celebration cake on page 145, using a rectangular, 11 x 8 1/2-inch/28 x 22cm non-stick cake pan. Bake for 15 minutes, until golden and springy to the touch. Remove from the oven and leave to cool in the pan.

For the filling, whisk the cream until thick. In another bowl, whisk the ricotta and sugar together until creamy. Stir in the candied peel, chocolate and thickened cream. Cover and refrigerate for at least 30 minutes.

Line 2 1/2-inch/12 x 6cm ovenproof bowls with plastic wrap. Dust a work surface with plenty of sifted icing sugar and roll out the marzipan to a thickness of 1/8 inch/3mm. Using a 4-inch/10cm cutter, cut out 12 rounds. Line the plastic wrapped bowls with the marzipan rounds. Cut 12 pieces of the cooled sponge in the same way and place on top of the marzipan. Brush the sponge with Marsala, then divide the filling betweeen the bowls.

Using a 1 1/2-inch/4cm cutter, cut out 12 rounds from the remaining sponge and place on top of the filling, pressing gently. Brush with the remaining Marsala. Reroll the marzipan if necessary, cut out rounds and place on top, then fold the plastic wrap over to seal. Refrigerate for at least 2 hours, or until set.

Remove each *cassata* from the fridge, loosen the plastic wrap and tip upside-down to unmould. Remove the plastic wrap, transfer to a serving dish and decorate with sugared flowers, silver balls, angelica or candied peel.

Torta di Paolo

Paolo's cake

- - - - - - - - - - - - - - - - -

SERVES 6

scant 1 cup/200g unsalted butter,
melted, plus extra to grease

4 eggs, separated

1 cup caster/200g (superfine) sugar

1 vanilla pod

1 cup/150g all-purpose flour

$1/3$ cup/50g cornstarch

1 tsp baking powder

a pinch of salt

finely grated zest of 1 unwaxed lemon

confectioners' sugar, sifted, to dust

- - - - - - - - - - - - - - - - -

My good friend Paolo is an expert at making this traditional Italian cake, commonly known as *Torta Margherita* or *Paradiso*. This is his mother's recipe, which he has been recreating ever since he left home. Each time he makes this cake and brings it round, it disappears in no time. Simple to make, it is ideal with a cup of tea or even with a glass of Vin Santo after dinner.

Preheat the oven to 350°F/180°C/gas mark 4. Grease a round, $8^{1}/_{2}$ inch/22cm diameter loose-bottomed cake pan with butter, then line with non-stick greaseproof paper.

Whisk together the egg yolks and sugar in a large bowl until almost white. Split the vanilla pod with a sharp knife and scoop out the seeds with the tip of the knife, then add them to the bowl. Sift in the flour, cornstarch, baking powder and salt and gradually fold them in. Mix in the melted butter and lemon zest.

Whisk the egg whites in a clean, glass bowl until stiff peaks form, then gently fold into the egg yolk mixture.

Pour the mixture into the prepared pan and bake for 30–35 minutes, or until golden and springy to the touch. To check if the cake is cooked, insert a wooden skewer in the center – if it comes out clean the cake is ready; if not cook for a few minutes longer. Allow to cool in the pan. Unmold on to a plate and sprinkle with sifted confectioners' sugar.

PRESERVES

reserving food has always been important in my kitchen. It is a way of keeping the scents and flavors of produce long after it is in season. When I was a child, our store cupboard was always full of jars of preserved bell peppers, eggplants, zucchinis, mushrooms, green beans, artichokes, giardiniera (mixed vegetables), tomatoes, cherries, peaches and various fruit jams. We made most preserves ourselves, but friends and neighbors would come round with gifts of their own preserved goodies too.

The end of summer was a busy time for us, as the family prepared for the preservation of the beloved tomatoes. Kilos and kilos of them had to be bottled in order to give us a year-long supply. As well as bottling them, we sun-dried them and made concentrato (a very thick tomato paste). On balconies and terraces throughout our village, trays of salted tomatoes that had been sliced in half were dried in the hot sun. For the concentrato, they were put through a mincer to extract the pulp, which was then put in large, flat, terracotta dishes, covered with nets to keep the flies off, and placed in the sun. The mixture had to be stirred every couple of hours with a large wooden spoon and sprinkled with a little olive oil to prevent a crust from forming. The dishes were taken in at night and brought out again in the early morning for about 3 days, until the pulp had turned into a thick, delicious concentrate of pure tomato. It was then transferred into jars, drizzled with a little olive oil and stored. Just a little of this pure nectar was needed to make the most amazing ragù sauce for Sunday lunch. Not even the best shop-bought variety will ever match the flavor.

We preserved throughout the year, but mainly during spring, summer and fall. Eggplants, peppers, green beans and artichokes were placed in oil so that we could enjoy them later as antipasto or as a snack with bread. Peaches and cherries were preserved in syrup or alcohol or made into jam; figs were sun-dried and eaten at Christmas, and strawberries and end-of-summer berries were made into delicious jam to be eaten on bread or in my mother's crostate (tarts). We preserved all sorts of vegetables in pure wine vinegar to make our own version of giadiniera (see page 224). The vinegar was always our own, made with leftover wine that was poured into a large glass container to which a couple of pieces of dried pasta would be added – this helped to speed up the process of turning the wine into vinegar. We would leave the container open for about 20 days, gently shaking it daily, until the wine turned into the most pungent vinegar. The vinegar was then transferred into smaller bottles and sealed with a cork. I still do this at home today.

My mother even preserved her own tuna. When the fishermen caught this fish, word would spread around the village very quickly and housewives would assemble on the beach to buy pieces just for preserving. It involved a lengthy process of gently cooking the fish in salty water and then drying it, before placing it in jars with olive oil. The results were worthwhile and my mother made lots to keep in our store cupboard for quick, healthy meals. Families also preserved their own anchovies and sardines. A few years ago, when I was on holiday on the Sicilian island of Lipari, I preserved some anchovies and brought them home to enjoy at Christmas – the taste was amazing and reminded us of being back on the sunny island.

Preserving food doesn't just lock away its freshness; as you enjoy it, memories of where you were when you ate it, what time of year it was, who you were with and, maybe, even what you were talking or thinking about while you were doing the preserving will flood back.

We now find all sorts of produce all year round, but I still like to preserve. During autumn when we go mushroom-picking, and I love to preserve porcini (ceps) or chiodini (honeyfungus), which we enjoy having with our Christmas lunch antipasto, as well as giving away as presents. Liz's favorite is preserved eggplants and peppers, which again we enjoy as antipasto. My friend Paolo also loves to preserve, and at the end of summer, when his allotment flourishes, he comes bearing gifts of delicious fruit jams and mixed pickle. I hope this tradition does not die away; I certainly keep it alive and hope my young daughters will do the same when they are older.

Preserving basics

- Always use very fresh, good-quality fruit and vegetables that are in season.

- To sterilize jars: wash and thoroughly clean all the jars you are going to use, then rinse out with a little white wine vinegar. Leave to drain, then dry well. If you are using new jars, after washing them place in a large pan of boiling water and boil for a couple of minutes. Remove, drain and dry well.

- To pasteurize: once you have placed the preserves in jars, seal well, preferably using hermetically sealed lids. Wrap each jar in old kitchen cloths – this prevents it from breaking during boiling. Line a large pan with kitchen cloth. Place the wrapped jars in it and add enough cold water to cover them by 1 inch/3cm. Bring the water to a boil, then reduce the heat to medium and boil for the time stated in the recipe. Turn off the heat, but leave the jars in the water until it is cold. Remove the jars and unwrap, then dry with a clean cloth, label and place in the store cupboard.

12 long, thin, sweet green bell
peppers, about 12oz/350g in total

1¾ cups/400ml white wine
vinegar or preserving vinegar

20 black peppercorns

6 bay leaves

4 cups/1 liter olive oil
or good sunflower oil

for the filling

5½ oz/150–160g canned tuna in oil,
drained (keeping a little oil aside)

¾oz/20g capers, finely chopped

9 anchovy fillets in oil, drained
and finely chopped

Peperoni dolci ripieni sott'olio

Preserved filled sweet peppers

I love these long, thin, sweet green peppers, known as *friggitelli* in Campania. I usually buy them in Greek or Turkish shops and find they are slightly larger than the Italian ones; however, the sweet, delicate taste is similar and they are ideal for stuffing. When I find them, I buy lots, fill them with tuna and preserve them in oil so I can enjoy them as picked, as a little antipasto or light meal with bread. In Italy, my mother would fill and preserve tiny bell peppers at the end of summer.

Sterilize jars with a total volume of 8 cups/2 liters (see page 221) and dry thoroughly with a clean tea towel.

Using a small sharp knife, make a slit lengthways down one side of each pepper, then carefully remove the seeds and any white bits.

Place the vinegar in a pan and bring to a boil, then add a few peppers at a time and boil for 2 minutes, turning them over halfway through. Drain and leave to dry on kitchen towel.

Meanwhile, combine all the ingredients for the filling, adding a little of the tuna oil if necessary for binding.

Fill the peppers and place in the sterilized jars. Drop in the peppercorns and bay leaves and pour in the oil, making sure the peppers are covered. Secure with a vinegar-proof lid, and pasteurize for 30 minutes (see page 221). Label and store in a cool, dark, dry place for about 1 month before using. Once opened, store in the fridge.

Giardiniera

Mixed vegetable pickle

------- - -- --- --- -.-

MAKES ABOUT 2 X 1³/₄-CUP/450ML JARS

generous 1 cup/250ml white
wine vinegar

12 black peppercorns

2 cloves

4 bay leaves

1¹/₂ tsp salt

2 carrots, cut into chunks

1 celery heart, cut into chunks

5oz/140g cauliflower florets

4¹/₂oz/125g green beans, topped and
tailed and halved

1 small red bell pepper, deseeded and
cut into thin strips lengthways

1 small yellow bell pepper, deseeded
and cut into thin strips lengthways

5oz/140g baby (pearl) onions, peeled

5oz/140g eggplant,
peeled and cut into strips

3oz/85g green olives, pitted and halved

¹/₂ tsp dried oregano

4 red chillies (chiles), left whole

1¹/₂ cups/350ml olive oil, plus extra
to top up if necessary

------- --- --- --- --.-

Giardiniera is a classic Italian mixed vegetable pickle. It was traditionally made by farmers using the season's new vegetables. In many families it was traditional to fill a large *tinozza* (wooden container) with wine vinegar, and each day put in whatever vegetable you could find. The vinegar preserved them and we enjoyed them as pickled vegetables throughout the winter. At home, my mother would religiously make jars of *giardiniera* at the end of summer, which we would use to enhance the famous *rinforzo* (cauliflower) salad at Christmas.

Sterilize 2 x 1³/₄-cup/450ml jars (see page 221) and dry thoroughly with a clean tea towel.

Put a generous 1 cup/250ml water into a large pan and add the vinegar, peppercorns, cloves, bay leaves and salt. Bring to a boil. Add the carrots, celery and cauliflower, lower the heat slightly and simmer for 10 minutes. Remove with a slotted spoon and place on a clean tea towel to cool.

Add the green beans to the vinegar solution and cook for 4 minutes, then remove and leave to cool on the tea towel.

Add the peppers and onions and cook for 3 minutes, then transfer to the tea towel. Finally, add the eggplant and cook for 1 minute. Remove and leave all the vegetables to dry out and cool.

Put all the vegetables in a large bowl, add the olives, oregano, chillies and olive oil and mix. Leave to infuse for a couple of minutes, then carefully, without breaking the vegetables, fill the sterilized jars, pressing gently down with your fingers so the olive oil covers all the vegetables. Leave to rest for a minute and, if necessary, add some more oil. Seal with vinegar-proof lids and pasteurize for 30 minutes (see page 221). Leave to cool, then label and store in a cool, dry, dark cupboard for about 1 week before using. Once opened, store in the fridge.

2 large eggplants, about
2lb/900g total weight

salt

2³/₄ cups/700ml white wine vinegar or
preserving vinegar

1¹/₄ cups/300ml olive oil or good
sunflower oil, plus a little extra if
necessary to top up

2 garlic cloves, thinly sliced

¹/₂ large red chilli (chile), thinly sliced

2 tsp dried oregano

Melanzane sott'olio

Preserved eggplants

My family loves this tasty way of preserving eggplants. My wife Liz always makes a large quantity to be enjoyed at Christmas with our antipasto of cured meats. Everyone who tries them wants the recipe. My pregnant daughter-in-law, Judith, phoned one evening for the recipe in desperation to satisfy her craving! They really are tasty and make a delicious midnight snack on good country bread.

Sterilize 2 x 1³/₄-cup/400ml jars (see page 221) and dry thoroughly with a clean tea towel.

Peel the eggplants and cut lengthways into thin strips. Line a plastic container with the eggplant strips, sprinkle with a good handful of salt, then continue layering the eggplant and salt. Cover with greaseproof paper, place a weight on top and leave

for 1 hour. During this time, the eggplant will exude quite a bit of water. Squeeze out the excess liquid, return to the container and cover with the vinegar, then with the plastic wrap. Leave for a further 1 hour.

Drain the eggplant, squeezing out the excess vinegar with your hands. Place in a bowl with the oil, garlic, chilli and oregano and mix well, then fill the sterilized jars. Pack the eggplant snugly and, if necessary, top up with a little more oil. Secure with a vinegar-proof lid and, if you wish to keep them for some time, pasteurize for 20 minutes (see page 221). Otherwise, label and place in a cool, dry place for about 3 days before consuming. Once opened, store in the fridge.

Pomodori conservati a casa

Preserved tomatoes

MAKES ABOUT 4 X GENEROUS 2-CUP/500ML JARS

3lb 5oz/1.5kg tomatoes, preferably San Marzano or small plum tomatoes
a large handful of fresh basil leaves

Preserving tomatoes was an annual family ritual when I was a child – in fact, most people in our village would do it at the end of summer, when the local San Marzano tomato was plentiful. Lengthy preparations were made for it. I helped with gathering empty beer bottles and corks; a large table was set up in the garden with chairs around it for the production line to begin, and a big old oil drum was placed over a fire for the pasteurization process. We would preserve enough tomatoes to give us a year-long supply. Sometimes, when I'm lucky enough to get a glut of plum tomatoes at the end of summer, I like to carry on the tradition – of course, not in such a big way, but if I can get a dozen or so jars in my store cupboard, I'm happy.

Sterilize 4 x generous 2-cup/500ml jars (see page 221) and dry thoroughly with a clean tea towel.

Halve or quarter the tomatoes (depending on their size) and use them to fill the jars, adding the odd basil leaf here and there. As you do this, gently press the tomatoes down and pack them in. Seal with the lids and pasteurize for 30 minutes (see page 221)., then remove them from the pan, leave to cool, then label and store in a dark, dry cupboard. Once opened, store in the fridge.

MAKES 4 X 1¾-CUP/400ML JARS

2lb 4oz/1kg peaches, peeled, pitted
and cut into eighths

juice of 1 lemon

½ cup/100g caster
(superfine) sugar

Pesche sciroppate

Peaches in syrup

During summer, when peaches were plentiful, our family friend, Maria Gatto, who lived in the hills above Minori, would always preserve them. Her vast garden was full of fruit trees, vegetables and herbs – produce she would use in her cooking. She was always cooking for her elderly husband and 6 children. She would spend entire days in her kitchen and work late into the night to create wonderful recipes and make pots and pots of delicious preserves. Whenever my mother went to see her, she would return home laden with jars of Maria's specialities. We would enjoy her peaches later in the year, when they were no longer in season, and use them in cakes or simply enjoy them in their lovely syrup.

Sterilize 4 x 1¾-cup/400ml jars (see page 221) and dry thoroughly with a clean tea towel.

Put the peaches into a bowl with the lemon juice and set aside.

Heat generous 2 cups/500ml water in a saucepan with the sugar. Remove from the heat and leave to cool.

Drain the peaches and use them to fill the sterilized jars. Pour the cooled syrup over them, making sure you cover them completely. Secure with the lids.

Pasteurize for 1 minute (see page 221), then remove from the pan and leave to cool. Label and store in a cool, dry, dark cupboard until required. Once opened, store in the fridge.

Marmellata di fragole

Strawberry jam

This is my mom's strawberry jam, which she made each year in May when strawberries were plentiful. I would collect the small wild strawberries, *fragoline*, that covered the hills above Minori. I had to resist eating too many of them on the way home because if I didn't bring enough my mom wouldn't make her delicious jam. I loved to watch her make it and was sometimes allowed to stir it, but the best treat of all was that she always let me have some of it warm on bread to test. Once potted, the jam was stored in the cupboard and she would use it to fill her delicious *crostata* (see page 210). This is a really simple recipe, made in no time, and so much better and more nutritious than any shop-bought variety.

Sterilize 2 x generous 1-cup/250ml jars (see page 221) and dry thoroughly with a clean tea towel. Put a saucer in the freezer, for testing the jam later.

Place all the ingredients in a saucepan, bring to a boil and simmer on a medium heat for 20–30 minutes, stirring from time to time. To test if the jam is ready, place a little on a cold saucer – if it sets, it is ready.

Remove from the heat, fill the sterilized jars and seal with the lids. Pasteurize for 30 minutes (see page 221). Immediately place upside-down until cool. label and store in a cool, dry place and use when required. Once opened, store in the fridge.

MAKES 5 X 500ML/18FL OZ/GENEROUS 2-CUP JARS

3lb 5oz/1.5kg damsons

1 1/2 cups/300g caster (superfine) or granulated sugar

5 cloves

2 bay leaves

2 3/4 cups/700ml pure grain alcohol (available from good Italian delis)

Susine selvatiche sotto spirito

Damsons in alcohol

I was in the country with my friend Paolo, cutting branches for my walking sticks, when we spotted a tree full of damsons. Of course, we had to pick them and, once home, I decided to preserve them in alcohol like we used to do in Italy. With his share, Paolo made jam, which we now enjoy with toast for our breakfast.

Sterilize 5 x generous 2-cup/500ml jars (see page 221) and dry thoroughly with a clean tea towel.

Prick the damsons all over with a pin and set aside. Place 1 1/2 cups/350ml water in a saucepan with the sugar, cloves and bay leaves. Cook over a medium heat until the sugar has dissolved. Remove from the heat and stir in the alcohol.

Fill the sterilized jars with the damsons, pour the liquid over them, making sure you cover them completely, and leave for a couple of minutes until the bubbles subside. Secure with the lids, label and leave for 3 months in a cool, dry, dark place before using. Once opened, store in the fridge.

MAKES 2 X GENEROUS 2-CUP/
500ML JARS

1lb 2oz/500g good cherries

generous 1 cup/225g caster (superfine)
or granulated sugar

1¼ cups/300ml pure grain alcohol
(available from good
Italian delis)

Ciliegie sotto spirito

Cherries preserved in alcohol

Cherries are the first hint that summer really is on its way! I always look forward to seeing the trees in full bloom and the market stalls being piled high with the succulent fruit. Every year my father preserved cherries in alcohol so we could enjoy them later in the winter months. I do the same and look forward to opening a jar around Christmas time and enjoying a little taste of summer with a slice of cake.

Sterilize 2 x 2-cup/500ml jars (see page 221) and dry thoroughly with a clean tea towel. Put a saucer in the freezer, for testing the jam later.

Trim the cherry stems, leaving on about a quarter of their length. Prick the cherries all over with a pin.

Place 1¼ cups/300ml water in a saucepan with the sugar. Put over a medium heat and stir until the sugar has dissolved. Remove from the heat and stir in the alcohol.

Fill the sterilized jars with the cherries and pour in the liquid, making sure you cover them completelly. Leave to cool, then secure with the lids and label. Leave for about 3 months in a cool, dry, dark place before using. Once opened, store in the fridge.

Index

ACKNOWLEDGEMENTS

Liz Przybylski for ghostwriting the book and organizing me. Adriana for testing the recipes and cooking at the photo shoots. David Loftus for the outstanding photographs. Sara Mulvanny for the gorgeous illustrations. Georgina Hewitt for the art direction and design and Miranda Harvey for laying it all out. Paolo Baietti for helping at the photo shoots. Barbara for editing and correcting. Becca Spry at Pavilion for overseeing the project. Chloe, Olivia, Eoin Dylan and Freddie for being fabulous at the shoot. Luigi Bonomi, my agent.